Gooseberry Patch co.

Simple Joys
of Friendship

A Country Store In Your Mailbox ®

Gooseberry Patch
600 London Road
Department Book
Delaware, OH 43015

1·800·854·6673
gooseberrypatch.com

Copyright 2002, Gooseberry Patch 1-888052-98-8
First Printing, April, 2002

How To Subscribe

Would you like to receive
"A Country Store in Your Mailbox"®?
For a 2-year subscription to our 96-page
Gooseberry Patch catalog, simply send $3.00 to:

Gooseberry Patch
600 London Road
Delaware, OH 43015

Contents

Heart to Heart 5

Shared Joys 49

Remember When 115

Forever Friends 161

Friendship is the
golden thread
that ties the Heart
of all the world.

–John Evelyn

Dedication

This book is for everyone who loves memories, friends and food!

Appreciation

Thanks for sharing your sweet memories (and recipes!) with us...they're like a warm hug from a friend.

Heart
to
Heart

Sweet & tender memories...

I have a fond memory of a sweet, elderly neighbor and his wife. Earl was our closest neighbor and whenever my husband and I dropped by for a visit, we always ended up staying longer than we anticipated; we really enjoyed each other's company. Earl was a terrific candy maker and after several visits to his home, he told me I'd be invited to his next candy-making day so I could learn his special recipes.

One fall afternoon he invited me over; I hurried down with my 5-month-old son and listened and learned Earl's tips and secrets for perfect candy. He and his wife worked as a team, measuring, checking the candy and then checking it again. It wasn't many years later that Earl passed away, but his recipes live on. The memories of this candy are sweet, just like our neighbors, and it bridged the age differences between our families. Remember to share with neighbors and friends…that's what makes candy the sweetest.

Shawna Searle
Burley, ID

6

Heart to Heart

Earl's Caramel Corn

12-qts. popped popcorn
2 c. flaked coconut
2-1/2 c. water
3 c. sugar
2 c. brown sugar, packed
1-1/4 c. corn syrup

2 t. salt
4 c. Spanish peanuts
2 t. vanilla extract
1/2 c. butter
1/4 t. baking soda

Toss popcorn and coconut; place in a large roasting pan and set aside in a 250-degree oven to keep warm. Heat water, sugars and syrup in a heavy saucepan to soft-ball stage or 234 degrees on a candy thermometer. Add salt and peanuts; heat to soft-crack stage or 292 degrees on a candy thermometer. Remove from heat; add vanilla and butter, stirring until melted. Add baking soda; stir until creamy. Pour over warm popcorn mixture; toss until well coated. Spread on greased baking sheets to cool. Makes 12 quarts.

I am writing to honor the women in my life who have shaped me into who I am today and who I strive to become. Just as a successful recipe is a careful mix of ingredients, I believe that I am a mixture of all the women who have influenced my life. When I finished college, I moved from home to start my teaching career. I had never lived very far away from my mother, who was my best friend, and I was very homesick. A group of women teachers welcomed me with open arms. During my second year of teaching, my mother's breast cancer relapsed and, within several months, she passed away.

The outpouring of love these women showed me was overwhelming. They found countless ways to treat me as a daughter. Vickie Andrews, Pam Bushouse, Janeal Krehbiel, Jon Kay Murphy, Teri Oberzan and Jane Scarfe, you have all become a part of me. Someday I will have a daughter of my own and, in her eyes, I will see a reflection of all of you.

Melissa Wieczorek
Bloomington, IN

Heart to Heart

Chocolate-Covered Peanut Butter Balls

1/2 c. butter

12-oz. jar creamy peanut
butter

1-lb. pkg. powdered sugar

3-1/2 c. crispy rice cereal

1.55-oz. chocolate bar

24-oz. pkg. chocolate chips

1/4 bar paraffin wax, sliced
into small pieces

Melt butter and peanut butter together; remove from heat.
Add powdered sugar and cereal; mix with hands and form
into walnut-size balls. Place balls on baking sheet; chill for
1/2 hour. Melt chocolate bar, chips and paraffin wax in a
double boiler. Dip each ball in chocolate mixture; return
to baking sheet. Place in refrigerator to chill. Makes 4 to
5 dozen.

My best friend was Allie Cannon. We met in 1988 while I was in the U.S. Army stationed in California. Our daughters went to school together and we attended the same church. Both interested in crafts, Allie convinced me to take a woodcutting class on the base and I'm glad I did. Before we knew it, we were both garage crafters with our own saws and sanders! I retired in 1992 and settled in Utah, Allie moved to Virginia and then to Italy. Because she was helping plan her daughter's wedding while still in Italy, I was honored to be asked to go with her daughter to shop for a wedding dress. That Christmas, Allie sent me a bread maker as a thank you for all my help.

This past February, Allie died of congestive heart failure at the age of 46. She always referred to me as the sister she never had and I miss her so much. Nobody has ever showed me the love Allie did and I couldn't have had a better friend.

Barbara Sherman
Magna, UT

Heart to Heart

Cinnamon Rolls

1 c. warm water
2 T. margarine
1 t. salt
3 c. bread flour
1 T. instant yeast

1/4 c. sugar
1 t. lemon extract
1 T. margarine, melted
2 T. each sugar and
   cinnamon, mixed

Place first 7 ingredients in bread maker and process on dough cycle; the dough should cling together as it is mixing. After processing, roll out on a flat surface in a 15"x6" rectangle, about 1/4-inch thick. Spread melted margarine over dough. Generously sprinkle sugar and cinnamon mixture over dough. Roll up lengthwise; cut into one-inch slices. Place rolls on a greased baking sheet in a warm place; cover with a dish towel. Let dough double in bulk. Bake at 375 degrees for 10 to 15 minutes or until tops are lightly golden. Drizzle with glaze. Makes 10 to 12 rolls.

Glaze:

1-lb. pkg. powdered sugar
2 T. margarine

1/8 t. salt
Optional: orange juice

Mix sugar, margarine and salt until smooth. Thin with orange juice, if necessary.

Thirty years ago, while leafing through a magazine, I came across a listing of pen pals and decided to write. The young mom I chose had such a huge response that she couldn't answer every letter. She told me her name was Sharon Hansford and hoped I would write again. Soon, Sharon and I discovered how much we had in common and often our letters ranged from 10 to 24 pages! Quickly, 7 years had passed and we decided it was time to meet. Our husbands liked each other immediately and our kids became instant friends. We continued to visit each other's homes over the years and Sharon's Southern Banana Pudding was a special treat for us whenever we visited.

When my beloved husband, Bob, passed away suddenly, I was devastated. Sharon spent hours on the phone with me and was a pillar of strength during that difficult time. Now it's my turn to be supportive; Sharon is fighting breast cancer. Our pens keep flowing and our letters are longer than ever. Our friendship began in a simple way and it will last forever.

LaVerne Fang
Joliet, IL

Southern Banana Pudding

5-1/4 oz. pkg. instant
   vanilla pudding mix
3-3/4 c. milk
3 eggs, separated

2-1/2 doz. vanilla wafers
2 bananas, sliced
1/8 t. salt
1/3 c. sugar

Combine pudding mix, milk and egg yolks in a medium
saucepan; blend well. Stir over medium heat until mixture
comes to a full boil; set aside. Arrange a layer of vanilla
wafers in the bottom of an ungreased 2-quart baking dish;
add a layer of sliced bananas. Spoon a layer of pudding mix
over bananas. Continue layering, ending with pudding.
Using an electric mixer, beat egg whites and salt until
foamy; gradually add sugar. Beat at high speed until
mixture forms stiff, shiny peaks. Lightly pile meringue on
pudding, sealing edges well. Bake at 425 degrees for 5 to
10 minutes or until meringue is lightly browned. Serve
warm or chilled. Serves 12.

My friend Barbara was an angel on earth. She was a busy mom with 3 small children, one of whom was mentally and physically challenged. Despite this, she never complained and was always ready to help others in need.

She chaired many school and church committees and this easy casserole recipe quickly became a favorite for holiday luncheons. Sadly, Barbara was taken from us to be an angel in heaven but I will always remember her fondly.

Karen Thrash
Pompton Lakes, NJ

Heart to Heart

Barbara's Mission Casserole

Combine stuffing, butter and water; place into a ungreased 13"x9" baking dish. Layer chicken on top; set aside. In a separate bowl, mix soups, mayonnaise and lemon juice; spread evenly over chicken. Sprinkle with cheese. Cover with foil; bake at 350 degrees for one hour, removing foil the last 15 minutes. Serves 6 to 8.

Ingredients:

- 4 c. stuffing mix
- 1/2 c. butter, melted
- 1-1/2 c. water
- 4 c. chicken, cooked and cubed
- 10-3/4 oz. can cream of chicken soup
- 10-3/4 oz. can cream of celery soup
- 1/2 c. mayonnaise
- 1 T. lemon juice
- 1 c. shredded Cheddar cheese

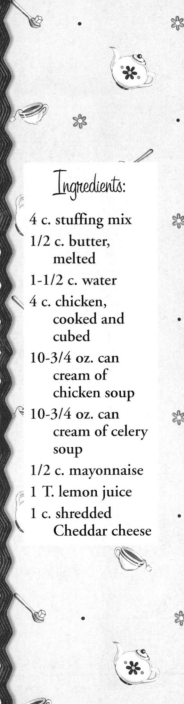

My mom was a very special and important person in my life. She was truly my best friend while I was growing up. Everyone loved her and she made our home a warm and comforting place every day…even more so during the holidays. Mom never let my brother or me forget the true meaning of Christmas or the importance of family & friends.

I remember how wonderful our home smelled during December when Mom made all the holiday goodies. I spent many hours by her side baking and talking things over. I can still see my sons in her kitchen, standing on chairs with aprons around their waists while they made cookies together. Even though Mom is no longer with us, her legacy lives on as we continue to enjoy her cookie baking tradition and wonderful recipes.

Patricia Lang
Prescott, AZ

Heart to Heart

Grandpa's Favorite Oatmeal Cookies

Beat first 6 ingredients together until creamy. Sift together flour, salt and baking soda; add to creamed mixture. Stir in oats until well blended. Drop by tablespoonfuls onto greased baking sheets. Bake at 350 degrees for 12 to 15 minutes. Makes 3 dozen.

Ingredients:

3/4 c. shortening

1 c. brown sugar, packed

1/2 c. sugar

1 egg

1/4 c. water

1 t. vanilla extract

1 c. all-purpose flour

1 t. salt

1/2 t. baking soda

3 c. quick-cooking oats, uncooked

Bobby was a childhood friend of my parents and I can't remember a time when he wasn't a part of our lives. He lived a few houses down the street from ours, so for him to stop in on his way home from work was just a part of each day. Bobby had been a cook in the Navy and he enjoyed sharing special recipes with us. One of his best was Norwegian Royal Crown Cookies...it just wasn't the holidays without them.

Although Bobby is no longer with us, I have years of wonderful memories and every time I make these cookies, I recall those very special times.

Bonnie Astuto
Dingmans Ferry, PA

Heart to Heart

Norwegian Royal Crown Cookies

1 c. butter
1/2 c. sugar
4 eggs, hard-boiled
1 t. almond extract

2 c. all-purpose flour, sifted
Optional: colored sugar

Cream butter until soft and fluffy; add sugar, blending well. Remove egg yolks from eggs, reserving whites for another recipe. Add egg yolks and almond extract; gradually blend in flour. Drop by rounded teaspoonfuls on an ungreased baking sheet; flatten each with a fork that has been dipped in water. Sprinkle with colored sugar, if desired. Bake at 375 degrees for 10 minutes. Makes 3 dozen.

Our daughter was diagnosed with cancer and, when she made it into remission, we couldn't have been happier. Since then, I have come to believe that the simple gestures we do for one another are more appreciated than anything we might buy.

Recently, a neighbor's son needed spinal surgery. He and his parents were in my thoughts since I knew how painful it was to watch a child go through something so serious. When they brought Mike home, I delivered homemade chicken soup, bread, applesauce and this chocolatey dessert. The thank-you note I received touched my heart and made me realize that just doing something simple from the heart is the greatest gift we can give.

Wendy Lee Paffenroth
Pine Island, NY

Heart to Heart

Brownie-Nut Pizza

2 21-oz. pkgs. brownie
  mix
2 8-oz. pkgs. cream cheese,
  softened
1/2 c. creamy peanut butter
1/2 c. sugar
2 t. vanilla extract

1 c. chocolate chips,
  divided
1/2 c. chopped walnuts
1/2 c. peanut butter chips
1 T. butter
1 T. milk

Prepare brownie mix according to package directions.
Spread mixture on a greased 16" pizza pan. Bake at
350 degrees for 15 minutes or until it tests done with a
toothpick; cool. Combine cream cheese, peanut butter,
sugar and vanilla; spread over brownie. Sprinkle 1/2 cup
chocolate chips, walnuts and peanut butter chips on top.
Melt together remaining chocolate chips, butter and milk;
drizzle over top of pizza. Set in refrigerator to cool for one
hour before serving. Serves 10 to 12.

My best friendship memory is of Mom and me baking my Grandmother's Butter Cookies. I was in grade school when we started this family tradition and, 24 years later, we still get together to make them.

Each of us mixes up a batch of dough to cut out and while they're baking, we make frosting and listen to Christmas carols. We've both been dealing with serious illnesses over the last few years but we still share good times together as mother and daughter, making great family memories that bring laughter and joy.

Robin Rinehart
Creston, OH

Heart to Heart

Grandmother's Butter Cookies

1 c. butter
1-1/2 c. sugar
3 eggs, beaten
3 c. all-purpose flour

3 t. baking powder
1/2 t. salt
1 T. vanilla extract
1 T. milk

Cream butter and sugar in a large mixing bowl; gradually mix in eggs. Sift together dry ingredients; add to mix. Stir in vanilla and milk to form dough; chill for one hour. On a floured surface, roll out dough to 1/8-inch thickness and cut with cookie cutters. Place on an ungreased baking sheet; bake at 400 degrees for 6 to 8 minutes. Makes 3 to 4 dozen.

When you look at
your life,
the greatest Happinesses
are family Happinesses.

-Dr. Joyce Brothers

My very best friend, Mary, is an old-fashioned Minnesota girl and she's helped me through the roughest of times. When Dad was struggling with cancer, she sent me the most beautiful cards and music. These gifts helped me realize all I had to be thankful for, even though Dad wasn't well.

Mary also knits the most beautiful handmade socks. When Dad became ill, I received my first pair and they quickly became my favorite gift. She had given a little of herself to ease my pain and warm my heart. The day he passed away, I was at her door very early in the morning. She greeted me with a warm hug and a shoulder to cry on. She presented me with another pair of handmade socks. This gesture, along with her enduring friendship, has made me realize how very lucky I am.

Valerie Duggan
Sutton, MA

Heart to Heart

Fudgy Brownie Cake

Combine cake and pudding mix in a greased 13"x9" baking dish. Mix in eggs, oil and chocolate chips. Bake at 350 degrees for 30 minutes or until tests done with a toothpick. Makes 10 to 12 servings.

Ingredients:

- 18-1/2 oz. pkg. yellow cake mix
- 3.9-oz. pkg. instant chocolate pudding mix
- 4 eggs
- 1-1/4 c. oil
- 1 c. chocolate chips

As long as I can remember, Mom made fudge each Christmas. This fudge was a labor of love and I didn't realize how special this treat was to me until it was only a memory.

My mother died when I was only 25 years old and, unfortunately, I hadn't developed a love for recipes handed down. Three years ago, a dear friend called and said she had something that belonged to my mother. It was a tin that Mom had filled with fudge the last year she made it, along with the recipe! What a treasure it is to my family and me.

Debbie Wood
Salem, VA

Nadine's Fudge

2 c. sugar	2/3 c. milk
1/3 c. baking cocoa	2 T. margarine
2 T. corn syrup	1 t. vanilla extract

Combine first 4 ingredients in a saucepan, stirring until well blended; remove from heat. Add vanilla and margarine; beat until the shine is gone. Pour into a buttered 8"x8" pan, cool and cut into squares. Makes 2 dozen.

I treasure the time spent with my best friend from the first grade. We shared all our years in school, our first dates, proms, holidays and our first children. Growing up, I couldn't wait to share our Christmas gifts and her mom's Christmas candy. We'd sneak in the fridge and eat it until we couldn't eat any more!

I miss Connie; she was killed in an automobile accident a few days after Christmas and since then, her mother has passed away too. Every year at Christmas, I put a quilt Connie made for me on the dining room table and make my favorite candy in her and her mother's memories.

Connie Bryant
Wallingford, KY

Heart to Heart

Christmas Balls

Mix together margarine, coconut, sugar and milk. Form mixture into walnut-size balls; chill. In a double boiler, melt chocolate and paraffin wax together. Using toothpicks, dip balls into chocolate mix; let cool on wax paper. Makes 3 to 4 dozen.

Ingredients:

- 1/4 c. margarine
- 1/2 lb. flaked coconut
- 2 c. powdered sugar
- 1 t. milk
- 6-oz. pkg. chocolate chips
- 1/4 bar paraffin wax

Mid was one of my best friends, despite a 53-year age difference. Our friendship started over our love of crafting and it blossomed for years.

May Day was "our" day and each year, my girls and I made a May basket and hung it on her door. When we moved 6 miles away, she was sure the previous year was the last time she'd receive a May basket. Of course it wasn't and the baskets continued. One April, her health began to fail. When May Day came, I made her a lovely basket, as usual. Her husband took it to her and told her who it was from, but she knew who had brought it. She passed away that afternoon.

Carol Canier
Savanna, IL

Heart to Heart

Mid's Imperial Cookies

Cream margarine; mix in remaining ingredients. Refrigerate until well chilled. Shape dough into walnut-size balls; flatten with a fork on an ungreased baking sheet. Bake at 375 degrees for 8 to 10 minutes. Makes 5 dozen.

Ingredients:

1 c. margarine
1/2 c. sugar
1 t. vanilla extract
2 c. all-purpose flour

31

I lived next door to Miss Edna and she was the sweetest little old lady around! I could always tell when she was baking her homemade bread...the aroma was heavenly! Each time she made it, she'd bring a loaf to share with our family.

Since I've always wanted to learn to make homemade bread, I asked her to teach me. She agreed and told me to come over anytime. We just had a ball that day in her kitchen and I'll never forget all that she taught me.

It was a sad day for our family when Miss Edna passed away. Whenever I make these delicious rolls, I look back on my memories of the sweetest little old lady around and remember her kindness. Even though she's gone, she'll always be in my heart.

Dianne Gregory
Sheridan, AR

Heart to Heart

Old-Fashioned Yeast Rolls

2 pkgs. active dry yeast
1/3 c. warm water
1 c. butter
1-1/2 c. milk

5 c. all-purpose flour
1/2 c. sugar
1 t. salt
2 eggs, beaten

Dissolve yeast in water; set aside. Over low heat, combine butter and milk until melted. In a separate bowl, mix flour, sugar and salt; stir in milk mixture. Add eggs, mixing well; add yeast mixture to form a dough. Knead on a floured surface until smooth and elastic. Place in a greased bowl, turning to coat the surface. In a warm place, cover and let dough double in bulk; punch dough down. Shape into rolls and arrange in a buttered and floured 13"x9" baking pan. Cover and let dough double in bulk. Bake at 400 degrees for 15 to 20 minutes or until golden. Makes 3 dozen.

The Best Antiques Are Old Friends.

One of my favorite memories is about my sister-in-law, a dear friend. She was stationed in California with her husband who was in the Navy and, even though we talked frequently, I missed having her there in person. One year when they came for a holiday visit, I was determined to make it special. We even got our Christmas decorations up in record time!

After dining out and driving around to enjoy the holiday lights, we came home, got comfy and stayed up until the wee hours of the morning talking, laughing, crying and feasting on goodies including Apple Custard Pie. Time passed too quickly and soon we were at the family celebration the next day. It was special to have them all to ourselves for that one evening. Sadly, my sister-in-law died of colon cancer a year and a half later, but when I think of her I remember friendship, laughter and her vibrant spirit.

Marissa Endicott
Mercerville, NJ

Heart to Heart

Apple Custard Pie

1 T. cinnamon

3/4 c. sugar

9-inch frozen pie crust, thawed

3 to 4 baking apples, cored, peeled and thinly sliced

2 eggs, beaten

1 c. whipping cream

Combine cinnamon and sugar. Pierce the pie crust bottom with a fork; lightly dust bottom with cinnamon-sugar mix. Alternate layers of apple slices and cinnamon-sugar mix until all apples are used. In a separate bowl, combine eggs and cream; pour over apple slices; sprinkle top with remaining cinnamon-sugar mix. Place pie on an ungreased baking sheet; bake at 450 degrees for 15 minutes. Reduce heat to 350 degrees and continue baking for 10 to 15 minutes or until custard sets. Serves 6 to 8.

This scone recipe is one I've shared for years over a cup of tea with my closest friends. We all had babies and every couple of weeks, when our husbands were traveling, we'd get together to share our stories, faith, frustrations and always something yummy to eat.

One of my dear friends has since lost her battle with breast cancer so memories of those special times are especially meaningful.

Karen O'Brien
Midlothian, VA

Heart to Heart

Karen's Raisin Scones

2 c. all-purpose flour
1/4 c. sugar
1 T. baking powder
1/2 c. butter

1/4 c. raisins
1 c. whipping cream
1 egg, beaten

Combine flour, sugar and baking powder; cut in butter until mixture resembles fine crumbs. Add raisins and whipping cream; mix well. Form dough into a ball; roll out 1/2-inch thick and cut into desired sizes. Place on an ungreased baking sheet; brush the top of each scone with egg. Bake at 350 degrees for 15 minutes. Makes 12 servings.

Some of my best memories are of Mom's kitchen...mouth-watering aromas and the sense of family that I always got from being there. Although we tried to gather for supper during the week, Sundays were always the big family get-together. It was a time set aside for catching up with everyone and just knowing how blessed we were to have each other.

Things aren't quite the same now that we're all married with families of our own and my father is no longer with us. I'll always cherish those special Sundays, the laughter and the closeness.

Sue Hogarth
Lancaster, CA

Heart to Heart

Sunday Chicken

In a 2-quart casserole dish, blend broth into soup. Mix in remaining ingredients, except almonds. Bake at 325 degrees for 40 minutes. Sprinkle with almonds before serving. Serves 4.

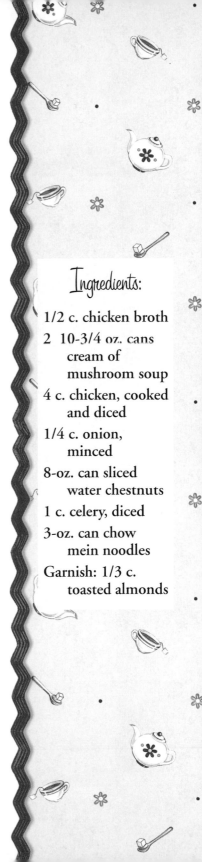

Ingredients:

- 1/2 c. chicken broth
- 2 10-3/4 oz. cans cream of mushroom soup
- 4 c. chicken, cooked and diced
- 1/4 c. onion, minced
- 8-oz. can sliced water chestnuts
- 1 c. celery, diced
- 3-oz. can chow mein noodles
- Garnish: 1/3 c. toasted almonds

A family is a circle of Friends who Love you.

—Unknown

What better friends to have while growing up than Mom & Dad? Mom worked some Saturdays when we were young, so it was Pop who always made lunch. One Saturday morning Pop took out his trusty skillet and my brother, Bob and I were excited because we knew he was going to make his Goody Potatoes!

There was a very large thunderstorm while he was making lunch and Bob and I began to be afraid. But Pop looked at us with a twinkle in his blue eyes and said, "Don't be afraid, it's only the angels in heaven bowling." Now every time we have a thunderstorm, I think of angels bowling and Pop's potatoes.

Dianne Selep
Warren, OH

Heart to Heart

Pop's Goody Potatoes

2 T. oil

4 c. mashed potatoes

salt and pepper to taste

4 eggs

Over medium heat, coat the bottom of a skillet with oil; add mashed potatoes, salt and pepper. In the center of potatoes, add eggs and stir well until the potatoes have a thin golden brown crust. Makes 4 servings.

Every Christmas, Grandma loved to get together with her family to make Pumpkin Rolls. We always gathered at her home to make these treats. We worked together, placed them in the oven, and before long the whole kitchen was filled with a wonderful aroma. We'd laugh and listen to Christmas music and talk about past holidays. Grandma went to heaven last January. Now, she can cook to her heart's content and never worry about getting tired or missing out on a word that might be said.

Because she taught us the value of family and giving, we carry on her tradition…my mother, daughter, niece and I gather to make Pumpkin Rolls. We listen to music, laugh and talk about Christmases past. I am so lucky to have these members of my family as my best friends.

Liz Hall
Worthington, IN

Heart to Heart

Pumpkin Roll

3 eggs
1 c. sugar
2/3 c. canned pumpkin
1 t. lemon juice
3/4 c. all-purpose flour

2 t. cinnamon
1 t. baking powder
1/2 t. salt
1/4 t. nutmeg
Garnish: powdered sugar

In a mixing bowl, beat eggs on high for 5 minutes. Gradually beat in sugar until thick and lemon-colored. Add pumpkin and lemon juice. In a separate bowl, combine remaining ingredients; fold into pumpkin mixture. Line a greased 15"x10"x1" with wax paper; grease and flour paper. Spread batter into pan. Bake at 375 degrees for 15 minutes or until cake springs back when lightly touched. Immediately turn out onto a towel dusted with powdered sugar. Peel wax paper off cake; roll cake up in towel, starting with the short end; cool. Carefully unroll cake. Spread filling over cake to one inch of edges; roll up again. Cover and chill until serving. Makes about 10 servings.

Cream Cheese Filling:

2 3-oz. pkgs. cream cheese, softened
1 c. powdered sugar

1/4 c. butter, softened
1/2 t. vanilla extract

Beat all ingredients together until fluffy.

43

A happy memory for me is of Mom making a batch of caramel corn and hot chocolate every fall or winter. Sometimes she'd make them both on the night we planned to decorate our Christmas tree…a snack to keep us from eating the plain popcorn that we were supposed to string for the tree garland! We lost Mom last year at the young age of 63; her recipes mean so much now.

Beth Goblirsch
Minneapolis, MN

Heart to Heart

Creamy Hot Chocolate Mix

25.6-oz. box powdered
milk

1-lb. box chocolate
drink mix

6-oz. jar powdered
non-dairy creamer

1 c. sugar

Mix all ingredients together and store in a tightly
closed container. To make one cup hot chocolate,
place 3 to 4 tablespoons mix in a mug and add one
cup boiling water.

My best and most-cherished friend in the whole world was my mom. We always shared so much fun and love in our kitchen. In the 1950's, there wasn't a lot of money for extras, but she could come up with the best treats for our family. These Creme Puffs were one of our favorites.

Her family was so important to her and she taught me so much about life with that old wooden spoon always in her hand. We went from talking about friends, to my first kiss, to getting married, and her favorite, telling her she was going to be a grandma.

Even though Mom has passed away now, when I stand in her kitchen I can hear her words; all with that wooden spoon in hand. Oh, if that spoon could talk.

Cynthia Strickland
Appleton, NY

Heart to Heart

Mom's Creme Puffs

3-1/2 oz. pkg. instant
    vanilla pudding mix
1 c. water
1/2 c. butter

1 c. all-purpose flour
4 eggs
Garnish: powdered sugar

Prepare pudding according to package directions; place
in refrigerator to chill. Combine water and butter in a
saucepan; heat to a boil. Stir in flour, beating continuously
for one minute. Remove from heat and beat in eggs until
smooth. Drop by tablespoonfuls onto ungreased baking
sheets. Bake at 400 degrees for 45 to 50 minutes or until
light golden. Remove from oven and allow to cool. Cut out
a small circular piece from the top of each puff. Fill each
with chilled pudding and replace top. Sprinkle with
powdered sugar. Makes one dozen.

Come and share
my pot of tea,
my home is warm and
my friendship's free.

-Unknown

Notes

Shared Joys

Celebrating special times...

My grandmother, Lila Reese, is one of my very best friends. She is 97 years old and still follows all sporting events, loves shopping and prays daily for her family. She has many, many young friends who sit at her feet and we all want to be just like her when we grow old. She taught my mother how to make this sweet treat…passed down from my great-grandmother, Alice King.

Kary Ross
Searcy, AR

Friendship

Shared Joys

Lila's Lemon Meringue Pie

3 eggs, separated
zest and juice from
   one lemon
1 c. sugar

2 to 3 T. all-purpose
   flour
1 c. milk
9-inch pie crust, baked

Beat egg yolks until thick; reserve egg whites for meringue. Stir in lemon zest and juice; place mixture in a double boiler. Add sugar, flour and milk; cook until thick, stirring continuously. Pour into crust and top with meringue; bake at 400 degrees for 6 to 8 minutes until golden on top. Serves 6 to 8.

Meringue:

3 egg whites
1/4 t. cream of tartar

6 T. sugar
1/2 t. vanilla extract

Beat egg whites until stiff but not dry; add cream of tartar and sugar, one tablespoon at a time until sugar is dissolved. Beat in vanilla.

My friend Jodi and I share lots of great memories. We both have three children and, one summer day in July, we got together to let the kids and moms play. After we put the kids down for their naps, we kicked back and enjoyed the quiet. Since it was close to the 4th of July, we made patriotic wind chimes while watching Mr. Smith Goes to Washington. *For the whole afternoon, we enjoyed iced tea and our Summertime Pasta Salad and kept saying, "This is the life." We agreed to get together the next weekend. This time we watched* The Music Man *while making wooden flags.*

We both moved away after that summer and I miss Jodi dearly. Every 4th of July, I rent those movies and think of all the fun we had.

Elizabeth Furry
Minden, NV

Shared Joys

Summertime Pasta Salad

Mix pasta and dressing in a large mixing bowl. Add olives, cucumber, tomatoes and onions; toss. Pour onto a serving platter; top with cheese and crackers. Serves 4.

Ingredients:

16-oz. pkg. rotini pasta, cooked and drained

1/2 c. Italian dressing

2-1/4 oz. can sliced black olives

1 cucumber, peeled and sliced

2 tomatoes, sliced

1/2 onion, chopped

1 c. shredded Cheddar cheese

1 sleeve saltine crackers, crumbled

Each fall, close friends and I get together for what we call our "Cup of Cheer." Though busy schedules keep us from gathering during the year, this special time gives us the opportunity to renew our friendships. It's a delightful afternoon spent enjoying tea, chatting and making memories. As a special keepsake, we each exchange a special teacup and saucer we've found at tag sales or antique shops during the past year. After 5 years of this cherished tradition, we each have a lovely and unique collection of teacups that reminds us of a special time with dear friends.

Delinda Blakney
Bridgeview, IL

Shared Joys

Lemon Tea Loaf

Cream butter and sugar until fluffy; add eggs and beat well. Beat in buttermilk and lemon extract. Add baking powder and flour; mix well. Pour in a greased and floured 9"x5" loaf pan. Bake at 350 degrees for 40 to 45 minutes or until lightly golden. Remove from oven and brush lightly with lemonade concentrate; cool. Makes 6 to 8 servings.

Ingredients:

- 1/2 c. butter, softened
- 3/4 c. sugar
- 2 eggs
- 1 c. buttermilk
- 1/4 t. lemon extract
- 1/2 t. baking powder
- 2 c. all-purpose flour
- 2 T. frozen lemonade concentrate, thawed

Wherever you are
it is your friends
who make your world.

-William James

55

One damp and cold fall day, some friends and I made homemade apple butter outside in a large copper kettle over an open fire. We started early in the day and hours later, the apples had cooked down and were ready for canning. When my friend Marilyn and I had canned all the apple butter, she brought out a pan of Homemade Yeast Rolls. We spread them with leftover apple butter and it was so good! Now, no matter when I make these rolls, I have such fond memories of that day.

Kathy Moser
New Albany, IN

Shared Joys

Homemade Yeast Rolls

Combine 2 cups of flour, yeast, sugar and salt in a mixing bowl. Add water, eggs, butter and one cup of flour; beat with an electric mixer for one minute. Add remaining flour; mix well. Turn dough out on floured board; knead for 5 to 10 minutes. Cover and let dough double in bulk, about 30 to 40 minutes; punch down. Shape into rolls. Place in a greased 13"x9" pan; let dough double in bulk. Bake at 350 degrees for 20 to 30 minutes. Oil tops of rolls while still warm. Makes 24 rolls.

Ingredients:

6 c. all-purpose
   flour, divided
2 pkgs. instant
   yeast
1/2 c. sugar
1-1/2 t. salt
1-1/2 c. hot water
2 eggs
1/2 c. butter,
   softened
2 T. oil

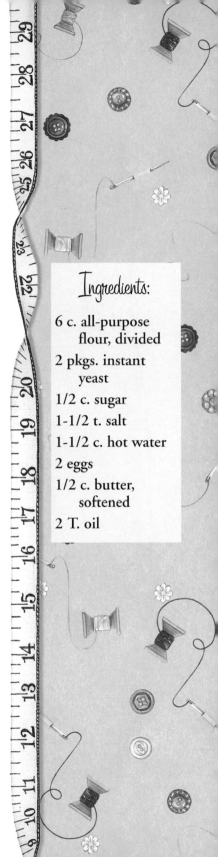

When we moved, I was feeling a little lonely and longing for some new friends. That's when I met Becky at church and was immediately drawn to her kind nature and sense of humor. She and I and both our little boys became the best of friends and it wasn't long before I felt like I really belonged in my new town.

A few years ago, at Christmastime, we started a new tradition. One of us will put on the Christmas music and brew a pot of coffee while the other begins the preparations for traditional Dutch pastries called Banket (pronounced bon-ket). For our families, they are the ultimate treat! You don't have to be Dutch to appreciate the flaky crust and tender almond filling. Whenever I taste one, I savor the sweetness of a treasured friendship.

Bonnie Zeilenga
DeMotte, IN

Shared Joys

Almond Banket

In a large mixing bowl, combine flour and salt; cut in butter to cornmeal consistency. Mix in water with a fork to form a ball. Cover and refrigerate dough overnight. In a separate bowl, grate almond paste on large part of grater; add 1-3/4 cups sugar and eggs. Cover and refrigerate filling overnight. Divide dough into 8 equal portions. On a floured surface, roll out 8 strips, 4 to 5 inches wide and about 13 inches long. Divide filling into 8 equal portions; rolling them into balls. Roll filling out like a pencil and place one on each pastry strip. Fold the dough ends toward the filling, then roll pastry so dough is completely enclosing the filling. Place seam-side down on ungreased baking sheets; brush tops with egg whites and sprinkle with remaining sugar. Using a fork, prick across the top of each pastry. Bake at 400 degrees for 25 to 30 minutes or until golden. Cut each roll into one-inch slices to serve. Makes 8 to 9 dozen.

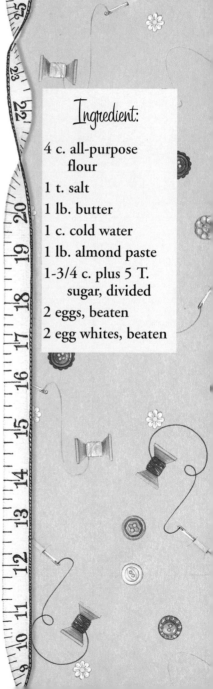

Ingredient:

- 4 c. all-purpose flour
- 1 t. salt
- 1 lb. butter
- 1 c. cold water
- 1 lb. almond paste
- 1-3/4 c. plus 5 T. sugar, divided
- 2 eggs, beaten
- 2 egg whites, beaten

Esther lived just a few houses down the street from my home when we were rambunctious 5-year-old kids. The long summer days seemed endless and I thought we would be together forever as we played the days away.

The years slipped by so quickly and we lost contact until I acquired Esther's e-mail address from her dear mother, Lois. Now we have renewed our friendship over the thousands of miles that part us between my home in Michigan and hers in New Zealand. The miles may be many, but each morning as I read her newsy letter I feel the closeness of our renewed friendship. As I type my letter back to her, I sip a cup of warm tea and tell her the happenings from home. The miles have disappeared and we are close again. We now trade recipes like this one for Cinnamon Chip cookies. It's so nice to try a recipe from another part of the world! Reading her letters feels as good as a loving hug.

Thais Menges
Three Rivers, MI

Shared Joys

Cinnamon Chip Cookies

1 c. butter
1 c. sugar
1/2 c. brown sugar, packed
3 eggs
2-1/2 to 3 c. all-purpose
    flour

1 t. baking soda
1 t. salt
10-oz. pkg. cinnamon chips
1/2 c. chopped walnuts

Combine butter, sugar and brown sugar in a large mixing bowl. Add eggs; mix until light in color. Sift together flour, baking soda and salt; gradually add to butter mixture, beating well. Stir in cinnamon chips and nuts. Drop by teaspoonfuls onto ungreased cookie sheets. Bake at 350 degrees for 10 to 12 minutes or until golden. Makes 2-1/2 to 3 dozen.

Pat and I have been friends since 9th grade. I can remember all the times staying overnight at her house, looking at make-up and walking her little sisters to the plaza for ice cream. I knew I could always count on her to listen to all my earth-shattering dilemmas, like when my father said he wouldn't wear a purple ruffled shirt for my wedding. (Purple ruffles were a '70's thing!)

We have shared, and continue to share, so many good times. Now we're in our 50's and are planning to travel to West Virginia for a quilt seminar. For a week we'll be together to reminisce and laugh about our "good old days."

Linda Black
Rootstown, OH

Shared Joys

Double Apple Cake

3 eggs
1 t. cinnamon
1/3 c. applesauce
18-1/2 oz. box yellow
   cake mix

1-1/3 c. water
1-1/2 c. apple, cored,
   peeled and chopped
Garnish: powdered
   sugar

Combine eggs, cinnamon and applesauce. Add cake
mix, water and apples; mix until moist. Pour into a
lightly greased 13"x9" baking dish. Bake at
350 degrees for 35 to 45 minutes. After cooling,
dust with powdered sugar. Makes 10 to 12 servings.

One of the joys I have in my life is a group of friends with whom I would love to grow old. I've only known them for a short period of time, but it seems like I have known them forever. We can laugh until our sides ache and cry until our tears have dried up. They are the kind of friends I can truly be myself around. Tracy, Dori, Terri, Katie and Debbie...I truly can't imagine my life without you in it!

We try to get together as often as time allows to do something fun, but whatever we do, there is usually food involved. I cherish these friendships and, in the next couple of weeks, one of these friends will be moving away. Hopefully, we will all remain close in heart. This recipe is one of the group's favorites and is always a hit whenever we meet.

Kathey Cox
Wildomar, CA

Shared Joys

Bread Bowl Dip

Cut a circle out of the top of the sourdough bread. Scoop out the inside, tearing into bite-sized pieces; reserve for dipping. In a medium mixing bowl, combine remaining ingredients; scoop into hollowed bread bowl. Bake at 350 degrees for one hour. Serves 8 to 10.

Ingredients:

- 1 loaf round sourdough bread
- 2 c. mayonnaise
- 3 cloves garlic minced
- 1/2 pkg. dry Italian dressing mix
- 1 c. Parmesan cheese, grated

Anne and my older sister are the only two friends who have known me all my life. Our families were neighbors and our homes were separated by only a vacant lot which was our playground, complete with a swing, a sandbox, and later, a Victory Garden. I was so sad when we were 6 or 7 years old and her family moved to the country. In those days, 30 miles seemed a lifetime away.

Through the years and over the miles, we've always kept in touch. Now, both Anne and I have found the best careers of our lives: retirement! We enjoy lunches that last long into the afternoon, seeking out special antiques and spoiling our grandchildren. Knowing Anne has made me a better person and a better cook. This Barley Casserole is a recipe Anne shared with me many, many years ago. Every time I serve it, I feel like I'm back in Anne's country kitchen.

Susan Martin
Portage, WI

Barley Casserole

1/2 c. butter
2 onions, coarsely chopped
3/4 lb. sliced mushrooms

1-1/2 c. barley, uncooked
2 c. chicken broth
salt and pepper to taste

Melt butter in saucepan; add onions, mushrooms and barley. Sauté 5 to 10 minutes, or until onions are tender. Turn into a 2-quart baking dish; blend in chicken broth, salt and pepper. Cover and bake at 350 degrees for 50 minutes. Uncover and bake an additional 15 to 20 minutes, or until liquid is absorbed. Serves 6.

Twenty-four years ago, Kelly's family moved from Massachusetts to Texas and became our neighbors. Before long, Kelly and I were best friends. Little did I know that the good times I had at Kelly's house would provide some of my fondest memories. They've even shaped the kind of home I try to create for my own children.

Kelly's mother was always baking something, filling the house with incredible aromas and a sense of warmth and coziness. I will never forget the Caramel Corn she used to make…it was better than anything store-bought! I make it now for my own children, remembering how Kelly and I would sit at the table, like they do now, laughing, playing board games and munching on her mother's caramel corn.

Cassie Maness
Alvin, TX

Shared Joys

Caramel Corn

Pour popcorn in an ungreased 13"x9" baking dish; set aside. In a saucepan, combine remaining ingredients; bring to a boil. Slowly pour mixture evenly over popcorn. Bake at 250 degrees for one hour, stirring every 15 minutes. Makes 6 quarts.

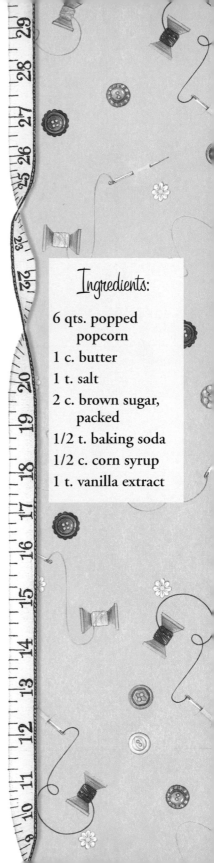

Ingredients:

- 6 qts. popped popcorn
- 1 c. butter
- 1 t. salt
- 2 c. brown sugar, packed
- 1/2 t. baking soda
- 1/2 c. corn syrup
- 1 t. vanilla extract

I would like to share the wonderful friendship I have with my granddaughter, Andrea. She began helping me in the kitchen by breaking the eggs when she was about 8 years old. She would always say, "Granny, be sure and wait for me to break the eggs." We would talk about what she and her friends had been doing and how her older brother, Bobby, had been "really mean" to her. I would tell her about cooking and writing down recipes with my own grandmother.

Last year she wanted to learn to make something "from scratch" and this Banana Pudding is her first "scratch" recipe. She's my only granddaughter and our friendship and the memories that we're making will always be very dear to me. I hope she will cherish our kitchen friendship too.

Glenda Fowler
Kaufman, TX

Shared Joys

Microwave Banana Pudding

1 c. sugar
4 T. cornstarch
1/8 t. salt
2 c. milk, divided
2 egg yolks, beaten

2 T. butter
1 t. vanilla extract
25 vanilla wafers
2 bananas, sliced

In a microwave-safe bowl, combine sugar, cornstarch and salt; mix in 1-1/2 cups of milk. Microwave on high for 5 minutes, whisking half way through. In a separate bowl, blend together egg yolks and remaining milk; add to microwaved mixture; whisk and microwave for 5 minutes, whisking half way through. Stir in butter and vanilla; cover with plastic wrap and cool. Place a layer of vanilla wafers in a 2-quart dish; cover with a layer of bananas; top with a layer of pudding. Repeat layering, ending with pudding. Serves 4 to 6.

My dear friend Dorothy just turned 81 years old and every minute I spend with her is an absolute delight! Dorothy grew up in London, England and she remembers historic events such as King George's funeral and Queen Elizabeth's coronation, as well as the night her house was bombed during World War II.

There are so many times Dorothy will say, "Won't you come in for a cup of tea and scones?" No matter how much I have to do or how rushed I am, I never refuse. She brews a pot of tea and I become lost in conversation. It's like having my dear grandmother for one more day, being immersed in a first-hand history lesson and visiting a friend from grade school all at the same time. I love to go places with her because she makes me see things in a whole different light. I suppose it's kind of odd that, at 33 years old, my best friend is 81, but with Dorothy, I just don't notice. She's done so much for me just by being my friend.

Dawne Strickland
Kingston, RI

Bran-Raisin Scones

1 egg, beaten	2 t. baking powder
2/3 c. buttermilk	1/2 t. cinnamon
1 c. wheat and barley cereal	1/4 t. salt
1-1/4 c. all-purpose flour	1/3 c. shortening
3 T. sugar	2/3 c. raisins

In a small bowl, stir together egg, buttermilk and cereal; let stand for 3 minutes until liquid is absorbed; set aside. In a large mixing bowl, combine flour, sugar, baking powder, cinnamon and salt; cut in shortening to cornmeal consistency. Add raisins, tossing until mixed. Make a well in the center of the dry mixture; pour in bran mixture. Using a fork, stir just until moistened. Turn dough out onto a lightly floured surface. Quickly knead dough by folding and pressing gently for 5 to 6 strokes. Pat dough into a 7-inch circle, 3/4-inch thick. Using a sharp knife, cut the circle into 12 wedges. Place wedges one inch apart on an ungreased baking sheet. Bake at 400 degrees for 10 minutes or until golden. Makes 12.

In 1996, our family moved from central Texas to the Rio Grande Valley. My husband is a Methodist pastor, so we go where we're needed. During our time there, I formed wonderful friendships with Sharon Waters, Merlene West and Susie Harrison. We'd go to movies, shopping, birthday celebrations and a long list of other adventures. We also began what has become our favorite tradition...a long weekend with just the four of us. Sharon has a lovely home on Lake Travis and every fall we visit her. Together we go shopping and antiquing, make quilts and take turns cooking our favorite recipes. One of our favorites is Sharon's Raspberry-Walnut Cake.

In 1999, we were transferred to another location, but we keep in touch with each other and look forward to our get-together each autumn. The four of us have a lasting bond. These friendships have been a tremendous source of joy and are among my greatest treasures.

Kay Sanderford
Victoria, TX

Raspberry-Walnut Cake

5 eggs, separated
2 c. sugar, divided
1 c. butter, softened
1/2 t. salt
1-1/2 t. vanilla extract
1 t. baking soda

1 c. buttermilk
2 c. flour
1-1/2 c. chopped walnuts, divided
1 c. raspberry preserves, strained and divided

Beat room temperature egg whites until soft peaks form. Add 1/2 cup sugar; beat until stiff peaks form. Cream butter, remaining sugar, salt and vanilla together. Blend in egg yolks, one at a time, until soft peaks form. Stir baking soda into buttermilk; add alternately with flour to butter mixture, beginning and ending with flour. Fold in egg white mixture; add one cup walnuts. Pour batter into 3 greased and floured 9" round cake pans. Bake at 325 degrees for 40 minutes; cool in pans for 5 to 10 minutes, then invert onto wire racks. Top 2 layers with 1/4 cup preserves and a thin layer of frosting; stack layers. Frost and spread preserves on top; sprinkle with walnuts. Serves 12.

Raspberry-Cream Cheese Frosting:

1/2 c. butter, softened
1/4 c. raspberry preserves, strained

12 oz. cream cheese, softened
1-1/2 t. vanilla extract
1-1/2 lbs. powdered sugar

Cream together first 4 ingredients; blend in powdered sugar.

Growing up in the 1950's, my aunt had a dairy farm in Mullica Hill, New Jersey. Auntie Re was more than an aunt, she was like a friend and grandmother all rolled into one. I spent many weekends at the farm and a few weeks in the summer too. My favorite memories are of cooking with my aunt. We made homemade grape jelly from grapes grown on the farm along with applesauce, apple pies and fritters.

Another favorite memory is of her Ginger Cookies. Whenever I'd visit, she'd ask if I'd like a cookie and out of the cupboard came a large tin filled with these soft cookies. To this day, I still make them for my family and remember enjoying them "down on the farm."

Diane Diggons
Barrington, NJ

Shared Joys

Ginger Cookies

Dissolve baking soda in hot water. Add all ingredients, except flour; beat well. Gradually blend in flour. Drop by teaspoonfuls on a greased baking sheet. Bake at 350 degrees for 10 to 12 minutes. Makes 2 to 3 dozen.

Ingredients:

1 t. baking soda
1/2 c. hot water
1/2 c. shortening
1 c. molasses
1 c. sugar
2 eggs
1/2 t. ground ginger
1/2 t. cinnamon
**4 to 4-1/2 c. all-
purpose flour**

My first friend, my mom, and I love to bake. I remember Mom and her sisters spending a whole day baking cookies. They always created a variety of treats and I loved helping to mix, roll and sprinkle the cookies before baking them. Some of the cookie recipes were only used at Christmas so they were always a special treat. One of those favorite recipes came from my Grandmother Mattie. Her Vanilla Drop Cookies are delicious!

Susan Biffignani
Fenton, MO

Shared Joys

Vanilla Drop Cookies

3/4 c. butter
1-1/4 c. sugar
2 eggs, beaten
1 t. vanilla extract

3 c. all-purpose flour
3 t. baking soda
3/4 t. salt
2/3 c. milk

In a mixing bowl, cream butter and sugar; add eggs, beating well. Add vanilla; set aside. In a separate bowl, combine flour, baking soda and salt; mix in milk. Gradually add milk mixture to butter mixture; chill for 3 to 4 hours. Drop by teaspoonfuls onto an ungreased baking sheet. Bake at 350 degrees for 6 minutes or until lightly golden. Makes 3 dozen.

My twin sister, Jennifer is my best friend. We live about 200 miles apart...exactly 3 hours and 40 minutes by car, but who's counting? When we get together, we spend most of our time in the kitchen trying new recipes or browsing through cookbooks looking for ones we'd like to try. One of our favorite recipes is for toffee. We've made it for gifts and always get requests for more. When my sister is with me, even the clean-up is fun!

Tonya Enich
Side Lake, MN

Shared Joys

Twins' Toffee

1-3/4 c. butter,
  softened
2 c. sugar
1 T. corn syrup

1 c. chopped pecans
1/4 t. salt
1-lb. chocolate almond
  bark

In a heavy saucepan, melt butter; add sugar and corn syrup. Continue cooking over medium heat to a soft-crack stage, or 295 degrees on a candy thermometer; remove from heat. Stir in pecans and salt; quickly pour onto a buttered 15"x10"x1" baking sheet and let stand for 5 minutes. Cut into squares. Melt chocolate in a double boiler, stirring often. Dip squares into coating; place on wax paper until set. Makes 16 to 20 servings.

81

I met my friend Vickie 10 years ago when we lived in Michigan. We felt an instant connection and have been best friends ever since. Our children were best friends too and whenever we got together, the kids would play outside while Vickie and I experimented with recipes. It was so wonderful to have a friend who was as passionate about cooking as I was!

A few years later, my husband and I decided to move closer to our families. Even though we're miles apart, Vickie and I still talk on the phone every week and visit once a year...it's as if we've never been apart. Over the years, we've baked many goodies together but this cookie recipe is the best ever! I hope you'll enjoy baking up a batch with your best friend.

Erica Wieschenberg
Towaco, NJ

Shared Joys

Chewy Chocolate Chip Cookies

Combine flour, cake flour, baking powder and baking soda in a medium mixing bowl; set aside. In a separate bowl, cream butter and sugars; add eggs and vanilla, mixing well. Gradually add flour mixture; stir in chocolate chips. Drop dough by rounded tablespoonfuls onto ungreased baking sheets. Bake at 375 degrees for 10 to 12 minutes or until lightly golden. Makes 5 dozen.

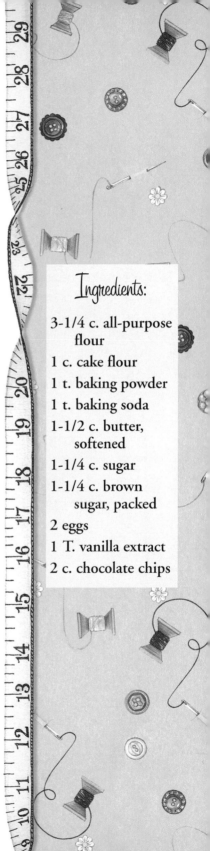

Ingredients:

- 3-1/4 c. all-purpose flour
- 1 c. cake flour
- 1 t. baking powder
- 1 t. baking soda
- 1-1/2 c. butter, softened
- 1-1/4 c. sugar
- 1-1/4 c. brown sugar, packed
- 2 eggs
- 1 T. vanilla extract
- 2 c. chocolate chips

Cyndie and I first met about 10 years ago when we worked together. She brought homemade salsa to share with us and it was delicious! She and I have both changed jobs since then but we're still good friends.

Every couple of months, we set aside an afternoon for lunch…which usually ends up being about 3 hours long! We eat, catch up with each other and find that, when the afternoon is over, we're both ready to face the world again until the next time we get together.

Christa Kerr
DuBois, PA

Shared Joys

Fresh Tomato Salsa

10 to 13 tomatoes, diced

2 4-oz. cans chopped green chilies

1 to 3 fresh jalapeño peppers, seeded and chopped

2 bunches green onions, finely chopped

2 t. cilantro

2 t. garlic powder

salt to taste

Combine all ingredients in a mixing bowl; mix gently. Allow salsa to stand for 30 minutes for flavors to blend. Makes 10 to 12 cups.

Friends are the
Sunshine of Life.

-John Hay

Denise and I were backyard neighbors when we had small children. We visited between our two homes each day...sharing treats, borrowing cups of sugar or babysitting. When the fence between our two yards went in, we even left an opening in it so we could continue our visits.

Denise was a much better cook than I was and she enjoyed trying new recipes. One day, I found a recipe for rolls that didn't require kneading. I made them and they were delicious! I shared the recipe with Denise...it was fool-proof and the cookbook was shared between our two homes for many years. Eventually, the cookbook became permanently wrinkled and stained on the roll recipe page but finally, we memorized the recipe. The cookbook was only one of many things we shared. Our friendship took us through many of life's experiences...we've laughed, cried and had so much fun. Denise is like a sister to me.

Gerri Klein Taylor
Draper, UT

Shared Joys

No-Knead Rolls

1-1/4 c. milk
1/4 c. sugar
1/4 c. shortening
1 t. salt
3-1/2 c. all-purpose flour,
    divided

1 pkg. instant yeast
1 egg
1/2 c. butter

Combine milk, sugar, shortening and salt in a saucepan; slowly heat until shortening begins to melt. Remove from heat and stir to melt shortening completely; set aside and let cool for several minutes. In a separate mixing bowl, combine 1-1/2 cups flour and yeast; stir in shortening mixture and beat in egg. Stir in remaining flour; add more flour if dough appears too sticky. Place dough in a large, buttered bowl, turn dough so all sides are buttered. Cover and let dough double in bulk; punch down. Divide dough in half; roll each into a 13-inch circle. Spread melted butter on each circle and cut each into 12 wedges; roll each piece to form a crescent. Place rolls on a greased baking sheet; cover and let double in bulk. Bake at 400 degrees for 20 minutes or until golden. Makes 2 dozen.

Seven of my dear friends get together every month and share a meal and a movie. The movie is usually something we can relate to and share special thoughts about. We take turns preparing the food...Apple Crisp Pizza is one of our very favorites. It's delicious! The combination of food, entertainment and love among friends is wonderful.

Carol Mackley
Manheim, PA

Shared Joys

Apple Crisp Pizza

9-inch refrigerated pie
crust, unbaked

2/3 c. sugar

1/2 c. plus 3 T. all-
purpose flour,
divided

2 t. cinnamon, divided

4 apples, cored peeled
and sliced

1/3 c. brown sugar

1/3 c. quick-cooking
oats, uncooked

1/4 c. butter, softened

Garnish: caramel
topping

Roll dough to fit a 12" pizza pan; flute edges.
Combine sugar, 3 tablespoons flour and one
teaspoon cinnamon in a mixing bowl; add apples,
tossing to cover. Arrange apples in a single, circular
layer to completely cover dough. Combine brown
sugar, oats and butter; sprinkle over apples. Bake at
350 degrees for 35 to 40 minutes or until apples are
tender. Remove from oven and drizzle with caramel
topping; serve warm. Serves 8 to 10.

Every year for the past 10 or 12 years, our family has spent four winter weekends at a state park with the family of one of my best friends. These weekends are for kicking back and relaxing.

Our favorite pastime is eating, which, of course, also involves cooking! The menu varies, depending on what diet someone happens to be on at the time. When the high-protein, low-carbohydrate diet was popular, our menu always included Egg Casserole. Good friends and good food…you can't get much better than that!

Sharon Goss
Greenfield, IN

Shared Joys

Egg Casserole

8-oz. ground sausage,
   browned, drippings
   reserved
1/4 c. green onion,
   finely chopped

8 eggs
1 c. milk
2-1/2 c. shredded
   Cheddar cheese,
   divided

Sauté onions in one tablespoon sausage drippings. In a mixing bowl, beat eggs with milk; stir in sausage, onions and 2 cups cheese. Pour into a lightly greased 8"x8" baking dish; bake uncovered at 350 degrees for 35 to 40 minutes. Sprinkle with remaining cheese and return to oven until cheese melts and casserole is set; serve immediately. Makes 4 to 6 servings.

Jane and I met 19 years ago in high school and have been best friends ever since. Her parents have both passed away and my mom has unofficially adopted her into our family. She truly has become like a sister to me. Jane lives in Texas but spends every Christmas with us. She makes one request every year she comes home…to have our Chicken-Broccoli Casserole on Christmas Eve.

This has become our tradition; we all gather at Mom's house and make Jane's favorite comfort food. After dinner, we each get to open one present…pajamas, of course! When I make this dish throughout the rest of the year, I think of Jane and wish she could be here to share it with me. I usually end up calling her while it's baking!

Mayumi Huffman
Gresham, OR

Shared Joys

Chicken-Broccoli Casserole

Layer chicken on the bottom of a lightly greased 13"x9" baking dish; top with broccoli. In a separate bowl, combine soup, milk and soy sauce; pour over broccoli. Sprinkle cheese over top. Bake at 350 degrees for 35 to 40 minutes or until bubbly. Sprinkle fried onions over top and bake for 5 minutes. Serves 6 to 8.

Ingredients:

- 2 c. cooked chicken, cubed
- 4 c. broccoli, chopped
- 10-3/4 oz. can cream of mushroom soup
- 12-oz. can evaporated milk
- 1 t. soy sauce
- 2 c. Cheddar cheese, grated
- 1 c. French-fried onions

93

Every year at Thanksgiving, my friend Melissa and I get together. We have a great time making homemade Christmas gifts for friends & family. In the past we've made peach-pepper jelly, salsa and blueberry marmalade. We love getting together every year in the kitchen to surprise everyone with our secret gifts.

Last year, we made Chef's Salt and even designed our own labels for the jars. It's great on grilled chicken, meat or vegetables. Everyone asked for "refills, please!"

Helene Hamilton
Hickory, NC

Shared Joys

Chef's Salt

1 c. sea salt
1 T. paprika
1 t. pepper

1 t. white pepper
1/4 to 1/2 t. garlic
powder

Combine all ingredients, mixing well. Store in an airtight container. Makes 1-1/4 cups.

Mom made many tasty dishes and her Corned Beef Casserole was always a favorite. When my best friend, Bonnie, spent the night, Mom would make this for dinner. Bonnie even asked for the recipe so she could share it with her mom!

As Bonnie and I got older and did more of the family cooking, we always made sure to include this casserole for dinner when we spent the night together. As we became mothers, you can be sure this was included in both our recipe collections. I wonder if Bonnie still makes it 35 years later? I do!

Janet Allen
Dalton Gardens, ID

Shared Joys

Mom's Corned Beef Casserole

Sauté onion in butter. Combine all remaining ingredients; place in a lightly greased 2-quart baking dish. Bake at 375 degrees for one hour. Serves 6.

Ingredients:

- 1/2 c. onion, chopped
- 2 T. butter
- 6-oz. pkg. macaroni, cooked
- 12-oz. can corned beef, sliced
- 1/2 lb. American cheese, cubed
- 10-3/4 oz. can cream of chicken soup
- 1-1/2 c. milk

My mother-in law, Ruth, was a special friend in my life. From the first day we met, she made me a part of her family. Each visit to her farmhouse home was a treat, as she cooked luscious recipes for her family. Her cookie recipe was a favorite for two reasons…it's so unique and was a favorite of her sister, Lizzie.

Ruth always stressed how important it is to keep family ties close. In fact, my husband's family reunion has been held on her farm for more than 105 years…the farm of over 80 acres is still in the family.

Marta May
Anderson, IN

Shared Joys

Aunt Lizzie's Forgotten Cookies

Preheat oven to 400 degrees. Beat egg whites until stiff; gradually add sugar. Mix in salt and vanilla; fold in nuts and chocolate chips. Drop by teaspoonfuls on an ungreased baking sheet. Turn oven off and immediately put cookies inside. Do not open until oven is cool, or leave overnight. Makes 4 to 6 dozen.

Ingredients:

2 egg whites
2/3 c. sugar
1/8 t. salt
1 t. vanilla extract
1 c. chopped pecans
6-oz. pkg.
    chocolate chips

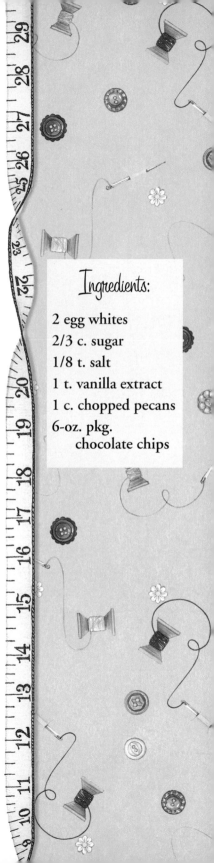

My favorite memory of friendship was a few years ago, when our family moved into a real "fixer-upper" during the month September. Being a teacher, I had to prepare for the school year while we were trying to fix up our broken-down house. Well, Christmas rolled around as we were putting in a new kitchen. The oven wasn't even hooked up until late Christmas Eve so I hadn't done any of the holiday baking I enjoy.

When my best friend, Sheila, showed up at my door with a beautifully decorated box of homemade treats, including her Fruit Jumbles, I was so surprised! She is truly a simple joy of friendship.

Elaine Remstein
Huntington Station, NY

Shared Joys

Fruit Jumbles

2 c. sugar
3-1/2 c. all-purpose
    flour
1/2 t. salt
1/2 t. baking soda
1/2 t. nutmeg

1/2 c. milk
1-1/2 t. lemon juice
1 c. butter, melted
2 eggs
1 c. chopped nuts
1 c. raisins, chopped

In a mixing bowl, sift first 5 ingredients together. Pour milk in a measuring cup, stir in lemon juice; set aside. In a separate bowl, combine butter, eggs, milk mixture, nuts and raisins; add to the dry mixture. Pour into a greased 13"x9" baking dish. Bake at 300 degrees for 45 minutes; cut into squares. Makes 2 dozen.

When friends meet,
hearts warm.

-English proverb

My life-long friend, Lee Ann, and I became acquainted in the fifth grade and quickly became the best of friends. If we weren't together, we were talking on the telephone, sharing all the wonderful things that only best friends can share.

Lee Ann's mom was an excellent cook and always made delightful treats for us. Soon, we were making them together.

Lee Ann was my matron of honor 48 years ago and, although she lives in Oregon, we still get together…and yes, we still end up in the kitchen preparing our old favorites like this delicious meat loaf.

Phyllis Gardner
Merced, CA

Shared Joys

Meat Loaf

Combine first 7 ingredients; mix well. Place in a lightly greased 9-1/2" pie plate. Mix tomato sauce and water; pour over top of loaf. Bake at 350 degrees for one hour. Serves 6 to 8.

There is only one thing better than making new friends and that is Keeping an old one.

-Elmer G. Letterman

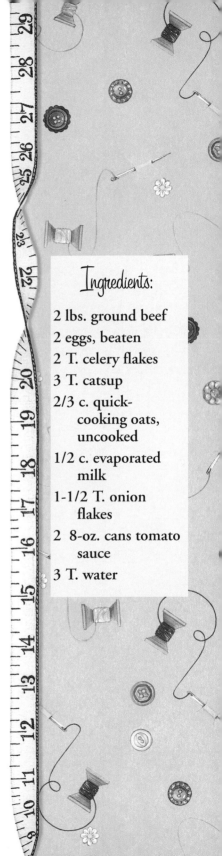

Ingredients:

2 lbs. ground beef
2 eggs, beaten
2 T. celery flakes
3 T. catsup
2/3 c. quick-cooking oats, uncooked
1/2 c. evaporated milk
1-1/2 T. onion flakes
2 8-oz. cans tomato sauce
3 T. water

My family and our best friends always get together the weekend after Thanksgiving in search of the perfect Christmas tree. We start off meeting for a hearty breakfast and put the ingredients for Shredded Beef Sandwiches in the slow cooker so it's ready for all the hungry elves when we return home.

Sometimes we hike for hours until we realize we saw the best tree in the very beginning of our search. Before we cut it down, we always pose for pictures. One year, as my friend Sandy and her husband, Jim, were bent over looking at the base of the tree, their 4 children bent over to see what they were looking at…I snapped a picture! I gave Sandy the picture with a note that said, "Wishing you nothing 'butt' a wonderful holiday!" It wouldn't be Christmas if I couldn't share it with my best friend.

Christine Richardson
Wadsworth, IL

Shared Joys

Shredded Beef Sandwiches

3 to 5-lb. pot roast
salt and pepper to taste
2 T. oil
2 c. water
1/2 c. red wine or beef broth

2 cubes chicken bullion per
   lb. of roast
2 onions, chopped
5 bay leaves
6 to 12 toasted rolls

Lightly season pot roast with salt and pepper; brown in
oil. Place roast in slow cooker and add remaining ingredients;
cook on high for 2 to 4 hours. Shred meat and serve on rolls.
Use remaining juice for dipping. Serves 6 to 12.

After graduating from college, I found that I could only "cook" frozen pizza. My idea of a gourmet meal was when I opened up a jar of spaghetti sauce and poured it over pasta. When I got my first job out of school, I met my dear friend, Barbara. Barb would often invite me over for dinner because she loved to cook. I was impressed with her cooking and thought I would give it a try and invite her over for dinner. Well, it didn't work out as I'd hoped. I burned dinner so we ordered out! That was the beginning of many cooking lessons and wonderful recipes Barb would share with me. One of our favorites has always been Mexican Lasagna…it's very easy to make.

Barb has instilled in me a love of cooking and I have no one else to thank but her. She's still the best cook, even though I continue to bake a frozen pizza now and then!

Gina Bass-Yurevich
Springfield, IL

Shared Joys

Mexican Lasagna

1 lb. ground beef
1/2 c. onion, chopped
15-oz. can refried beans
8-oz. can tomato sauce
4-oz. can chopped green
  chilies

1 pkg. taco seasoning
6 8-inch flour tortillas,
  halved
8-oz. pkg. shredded Cheddar
  cheese

In a large skillet, brown ground beef and onion; drain. Stir
in beans, tomato sauce, green chilies and taco seasoning.
Layer half of the tortillas on the bottom of an ungreased
13"x9" baking dish. Spread half the meat mixture over
tortillas and sprinkle with half the cheese. Repeat layers. Bake
at 350 degrees for 30 minutes; let stand 10 minutes before
serving. Makes 6 to 8 servings.

June and I grew up in the same small town of Berne, Indiana and have been close friends for years. While I was visiting, I took a peek in her recipe file and found a recipe for yummy-sounding potatoes. I jotted it down and, when I came home, I made them. I called June to chat and told her how much I loved her recipe, but she didn't know what I was talking about. It seemed June had never made this recipe.

We've had many laughs over the years about June's Potatoes and I keep telling her she should make them sometime! They're easy, come out perfect every time and disappear quickly. June's still never made them.

Marsha Schindler
Ft. Wayne, IN

108

Shared Joys

June's Potatoes

30-oz. pkg. frozen shredded
    hashbrowns, divided
12-oz. pkg. shredded sharp
    Cheddar cheese
2 c. whipping cream

1 t. salt
1 t. pepper
1/2 c. soft
    bread crumbs
2 T. butter, melted

Pour 3/4 hashbrowns into a large bowl; use remaining
hashbrowns for another recipe. In a lightly greased
2-1/2 quart baking dish, layer half the hashbrowns and top
with half the cheese; repeat layers. In a separate bowl,
combine whipping cream, salt and pepper; pour over
potatoes. Mix bread crumbs with butter and sprinkle on
top. Bake at 350 degrees for 45 minutes. Makes 8 to
10 servings.

Each day a group of friends and I always have lunch together. Our one rule? No one is allowed to talk about anything work-related!

Sometimes our conversations cover some odd topics. For instance, one day my friend Steve asked me what was my favorite vegetable. I answered, and then so did everyone else around the table. Finally, the question circled back around to Steve. When he was asked what his favorite vegetable was, he replied "Kielbasa!" We all laughed and Steve's never been able to live it down! This recipe's for Steve, with a favorite vegetable, potatoes, tossed in!

Holly Tefft
South Otselic, NY

Kielbasa & Potatoes

4 to 6 potatoes, peeled
  and cubed
2-lb. kielbasa, cubed
1 c. shredded Cheddar
  cheese

1 c. fresh Parmesan cheese,
  grated

Cook potatoes in boiling water until fork-tender. In a large
stockpot, combine potatoes, kielbasa, Cheddar cheese and
white sauce; heat over low heat until cheese is melted and
kielbasa is heated through. Remove from heat; stir in
Parmesan cheese. Serves 4 to 6.

White Sauce:

1-1/2 T. butter
1 T. cornstarch
1/2 t. salt

1/8 t. pepper
1 c. milk

Melt butter in saucepan; whisk in cornstarch, salt and
pepper. Gradually add milk. Heat to boiling for 2 minutes,
stirring occasionally.

My friend Sharon and I frequently go on trips to craft, quilt and cross-stitch shows. Anytime we are away, we look for restaurants that feature dishes with lots of garlic. One year, we went to Saratoga Springs, New York for a cross-stitch festival...we were in heaven! We started the day with garlic bagels topped with garlic cream cheese, had garlic in our Ceasar salads at lunch and found several restaurants that served garlic butter with bread for dinner. I am sure that we oozed garlic from every pore by the time we left.

Here is one of our favorite recipes with lots of garlic! You can add as much as your taste buds can stand!

Renee Smith
Sunbury, PA

Shared Joys

Tortellini Salad

Rinse tortellini with cold water. Combine first 6 ingredients in a large mixing bowl. In a separate bowl, mix oil and Italian dressing mix; add garlic and pour over pasta mixture. Add mayonnaise and Parmesan cheese; gently toss. Serves 4 to 6.

Ingredients:

1 lb. frozen tortellini, cooked
1/4 lb. crab meat
1/8 t. pepper
1/8 t. cayenne
1/8 t. dried parsley
1/8 t. dried oregano
3/4 c. oil
1 pkg. dry Italian dressing mix
1 T. garlic, minced
1/2 c. mayonnaise
1/2 c. grated Parmesan cheese

Notes

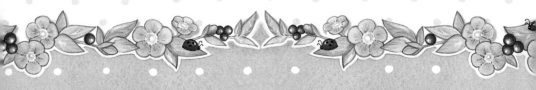

Remember
When

Having fun together...

For You!

It was the first day of school in 1988 when I took my children to the bus stop. Another mom was there waiting with her three children when a little girl looked down into the drainage grate and noticed a five-dollar bill laying at the bottom. As our children boarded the bus, I introduced myself to Theresa. Soon we were at her house looking for a broom. We taped a nail to the broom handle, went back to the grate and, using the broom, pulled out the money. We went to lunch on that five dollars and have been friends ever since! As our friendship developed, Theresa and I discovered we both love chocolate and we love making these brownies together whenever possible.

Suzanne Hickcox
Hagerstown, MD

Remember When

Sinfully Delicious Brownies

3 1-oz. squares
   unsweetened baking
   chocolate, melted
1/2 c. shortening
3 eggs
1-1/2 c. sugar

1/4 t. salt
1-1/2 t. vanilla extract
1 c. all-purpose flour
1-1/2 c. chopped
   walnuts
2 c. mini marshmallows

Combine all ingredients, except marshmallows;
pour into a greased 8"x8" baking dish. Bake at
325 degrees for 40 minutes. Sprinkle marshmallows
evenly on top of hot brownies; place back in oven
for 3 minutes. Cool. Spread topping over brownies;
refrigerate until top is firm. Cut into squares. Makes
12 to 16 servings.

Topping:

12-oz. pkg. chocolate
   chips
1 c. creamy peanut
   butter

1-1/2 c. crispy rice
   cereal

Combine chocolate chips and peanut butter in a
saucepan over low heat; stir until melted. Add cereal;
stir until blended.

For You!

One of my favorite things to do, whether it's summer or winter, is to have a tea party with friends! These get-togethers can be elegant or silly. One of my favorite memories is the year we all wore elaborate garden hats!

During these tea parties, we're all kids again…giggling, sharing secrets and making memories. Maple Nutty Scones is one of my favorite recipes to serve and share. Filled with crunchy walnuts and pecans, they always get rave reviews.

Rhonda Whetstone Neibauer
Wisconsin Rapids, WI

Remember When

Maple Nutty Scones

1 egg, beaten
1/2 c. buttermilk
1 t. vanilla extract
2 T. maple syrup
1 t. maple extract
3 c. all-purpose flour
1/2 c. quick-cooking
   oats, uncooked
2-1/2 t. baking powder
1/2 t. baking soda
1/2 t. salt
1/2 c. sugar
3/4 c. butter
1/2 c. chopped walnuts
1/2 c. chopped pecans

Mix first 5 ingredients; set aside. In a separate
mixing bowl, combine next 6 ingredients; cut in
butter until mixture reaches cornmeal consistency.
Stir in walnuts and pecans. Pour in egg mixture; stir
with a fork to make a soft dough. Turn out onto a
lightly floured board; knead to get a slightly uniform
dough. Shape into a circle 1/2-inch to 3/4-inch
thick; cut into 16 wedges. Place on a greased baking
sheet; bake at 425 degrees for 16 to 18 minutes or
until lightly golden. Makes 16.

For You!

Several summers ago, when my niece Carrie was spending a long weekend with me, we found an old-fashioned juicer at the local trash & treasure store. I explained to Carrie what the juicer was used for and then she suggested we make lemonade! When we returned home, we set about making our homemade lemonade. After rolling the lemons, juicing them and adding all the remaining ingredients, it was time for the final test.

Carrie took a sip, set the glass down and smiled. When I asked her what she thought, she said, "It's simply delicious!" That's how this recipe acquired its name, along with creating a great memory between an aunt and her special niece.

Debbie Reed
Wellsville, OH

Remember When

Simply Delicious Lemonade

To get as much juice as possible from the lemons and lime, roll them on a work surface using the palm of your hand and then slice each in half. If using an old-fashioned juicer, place each half on juicer, press down and rotate halves until no more juice can be extracted. If using an electric juicer, follow manufacturer's instructions. Strain juice and pour into a pitcher. Add sugar and water; stir well. Serves 4.

Ingredients:

3 lemons
1 lime
3/4 c. sugar
2-1/2 c. water

When I was about 14 years old, Mom finally let me make dinner on my own. I decided I would make Baked Chicken. Once I got all the ingredients out and started, Mom told me, "Don't forget to put aluminum foil on the bottom of the pan," and with that, she left me alone.

As I was putting the chicken in the oven, I carefully laid a piece of foil on the oven rack and set the baking dish on top of it. I thought it was very weird to put foil underneath the baking dish, but I figured Mom knew what she was talking about. An hour later when we both went in to check the chicken, Mom opened the oven door and started laughing so hard she almost fell onto the floor! I couldn't figure out why she was laughing until she told me she meant to put the foil underneath the chicken, not the pan. To this day, 13 years later, we still laugh about it!

Krystina Lesiak
Plymouth, MI

Remember When

Mom's Baked Chicken

1 egg
1/3 c. milk
2 c. bread crumbs

6 boneless, skinless chicken breasts
1 c. white wine

Mix together egg and milk in a small mixing bowl. Place bread crumbs into a separate bowl. Dip each chicken breast in egg mixture, then into bread crumbs. Arrange chicken breasts in a foil-lined 13"x9" baking dish; cover with aluminum foil. Bake at 250 degrees for one hour. Uncover; pour wine into dish and bake, uncovered for 15 to 20 minutes. Serves 6.

A good laugh,
is as good as
a prayer sometimes.

-L.M. Montgomery

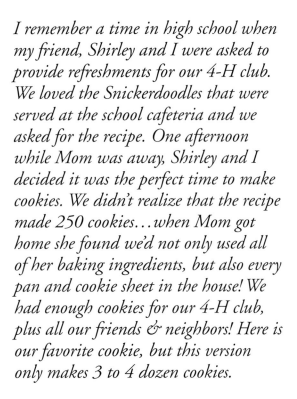

For You!

I remember a time in high school when my friend, Shirley and I were asked to provide refreshments for our 4-H club. We loved the Snickerdoodles that were served at the school cafeteria and we asked for the recipe. One afternoon while Mom was away, Shirley and I decided it was the perfect time to make cookies. We didn't realize that the recipe made 250 cookies…when Mom got home she found we'd not only used all of her baking ingredients, but also every pan and cookie sheet in the house! We had enough cookies for our 4-H club, plus all our friends & neighbors! Here is our favorite cookie, but this version only makes 3 to 4 dozen cookies.

Peg Baker
La Rue, OH

Remember When

Snickerdoodles

1/2 c. butter, softened
1/2 c. shortening
1-1/2 c. plus 2 T. sugar, divided
2 eggs
2 t. vanilla extract

2-3/4 c. all-purpose flour
2 t. cream of tartar
1 t. baking soda
1/4 t. salt
2 T. cinnamon

Cream together butter, shortening, 1-1/2 cups sugar, eggs and vanilla. Blend in flour, cream of tartar, baking soda and salt. Shape dough by rounded teaspoonfuls into balls. Mix remaining sugar and cinnamon in a custard cup. Roll balls of dough in mixture; place 2 inches apart on ungreased baking sheets. Bake at 400 degrees for 8 to 10 minutes; remove immediately from baking sheet to cool. Makes 3 dozen.

I met my best friend, Patty, in junior high school and we're still best friends today. We've gone through everything together...Sweet 16, graduation day, changes in hair color, marriages and our fast-approaching 40's. We've always said we're going to write a book of our life experiences and retire to a Caribbean island.

On a recent trip to Mexico, we enjoyed white sand, blue waters and lounging in beach chairs. If you could see a photo taken of us then, you'd see what looks like two women enjoying themselves on vacation, when actually it's two women previewing their retirement years with thoughts of being best friends when they are old and gray. That picture is framed and hanging in both our homes…it's a glimpse of what's to come. This recipe for Pineapple Cookies is reminiscent of that vacation spent on the beach sipping sweet pineapple drinks.

Marion Guay
Raymond, NH

Remember When

Pineapple Cookies

1-1/2 c. sugar
1 t. baking soda
2 eggs
16-oz. can crushed
    pineapple, drained

1 t. salt
1 t. vanilla extract
2/3 c. shortening, melted
3-1/2 c. all-purpose flour

Combine all ingredients. Drop by teaspoonfuls onto a greased baking sheet. Bake at 350 degrees for 10 minutes. Makes 2 to 3 dozen.

For You!

The year was 1985 and Christmas was only a couple of weeks away. My girlfriends all knew I made Stollen every year and they wanted to learn how to make it. So seven of us gathered early on Saturday morning and began...amid giggling and catching up and with two mixers kneading dough, our spirits were high. As we set aside dough to rise, we made more and more, and before we knew it, we had pans of dough on every available surface!

We spent the day baking and baking and finally by 8 p.m. we only had 3 more loaves to bake. We were giddy by now and the thought of Chinese take-out was unanimously approved. My friend's husband went to get dinner, but soon he called...his car stalled and so we went to rescue him. The day ended about midnight and home we went with our Stollen and memories we laugh about still.

Lynne Brown
Milwaukee, WI

Remember When

Christmas Stollen

2 pkgs. instant yeast
2 c. all-purpose flour, sifted
1/2 c. milk
1/2 c. sugar
1-1/2 t. salt
1/2 c. butter
3 eggs, beaten

1/2 c. seedless raisins
1/2 c. candied cherries, chopped
1/2 t. cardamom
1/2 c. citron
Garnish: powdered sugar

Combine yeast and flour in a large mixing bowl; set aside. In a saucepan, heat milk until very warm; stir in sugar, salt and butter; pour into dry ingredients, mixing well. Add eggs and remaining ingredients. Form into a stiff dough; add more flour if necessary. Knead dough for 10 minutes on a floured board; place in a greased bowl and cover. Place in a warm spot and let dough double in bulk.; punch down. Turn out dough onto a floured board, cover and let rest for 10 minutes. Divide dough into 3 equal parts; shape each into an 10"x8" oval, then fold lengthwise. Place loaves on greased baking sheets; let double in bulk. Bake at 350 degrees for 30 minutes. Dust with powdered sugar. Serves 15.

For You!

Twelve years ago, my husband and I were doing some remodeling in our basement. One Saturday afternoon, my 10-year-old niece, Julie, joined me to make Peanut Butter Balls. After mixing up the dough and carefully forming each ball, we then strategically placed them on a large cookie sheet which would be placed in the freezer down in our basement until they hardened.

After a few hours it was time to retrieve the Peanut Butter Balls to dip them in chocolate. We both went to the basement and somehow, while removing the cookie sheet from the freezer, it got off balance and they began rolling everywhere through all the saw dust on the floor! Needless to say, Julie and I still have a good laugh over this memory.

Jennifer Rick
Independence, MO

Remember When

Peanut Butter Balls

Mix together margarine, powdered sugar and peanut butter; add coconut, graham cracker crumbs and pecans. Roll into one-inch balls; freeze on an ungreased baking sheet. In a double boiler, melt chocolate chips and paraffin wax. Use toothpicks to dip balls into chocolate; set onto wax paper and store in refrigerator. Makes 3 dozen.

Ingredients:

1 c. margarine
1-lb. pkg. powdered sugar
1 c. creamy peanut butter
1 c. flaked coconut
1 c. graham cracker crumbs
1 c. chopped pecans
6-oz. pkg. chocolate chips
1/2 c. paraffin wax

Cooking may be as much a means of self-expression as any of the arts.

-Fannie Merritt Farmer

For You!

I've been making dolls for many years and am a member of a doll club. My friends and I share ideas and teach each other new skills all the time. The most memorable class was held at my house a few years ago.

We were making muslin dolls with painted arms, legs and heads. The dolls must be painted 4 or 5 times and allowed to dry between coats. Seven club members came and we were each making 4 dolls...that translates into 32 doll bodies, 64 arms and 64 legs. Now imagine a bright spring day and the need to hang these parts to dry between coats of paint. You guessed it, we hung them outside to dry on a clothesline. We had many people stop to stare; from a distance, it must have looked like little children were being strung up! We still laugh about that great day. When we have these marathon crafting sessions we always have terrific food and one of my favorites is this oh-so-simple salad.

Rhonda Crosby
Bakersfield, CA

132

Quick & Easy Vegetable Salad

2 15-1/4 oz. cans petite peas, drained

2 14-1/2 oz. cans whole green beans, drained

2 15-oz. cans shoepeg corn, drained

6 green onions, thinly sliced

4-oz. jar diced pimento

1 c. celery, chopped

1 c. sugar

1 c. white vinegar

1 c. oil

salt and pepper to taste

Combine all vegetables in a large bowl; set aside. Mix together sugar, vinegar and oil; pour over vegetables and stir. Add salt and pepper to taste; cover and refrigerate overnight. Serves 15 to 20.

For You!

I have a special friend who's always done favors for me for no special reason. When we met, we were both stay-at-home moms. I went back to work when my oldest child entered college and, needless to say, I didn't have the time to put into meal preparation as I had before.

One hectic night, my friend showed up on my doorstep. There was no special occasion...she just said she was thinking about me. Though her company was always welcome, she'd brought along a freshly baked pie, my family's favorite! Now that's a special friend.

Judy Bozarth
Fort Wayne, IN

Remember When

Fresh Rhubarb Pie

4 c. rhubarb, chopped

1-1/4 c. plus 1 T. sugar, divided

3 T. quick-cooking tapioca, uncooked

2 drops red food coloring

1/4 c. water

2 T. milk

Combine rhubarb, 1-1/4 cup sugar and tapioca. In a separate bowl, add food coloring to water; stir. Add water to rhubarb mixture; cover and let sit while preparing crust. Pour into crust and cover with top crust; trim and crimp the edges. Brush top crust with milk and sprinkle with remaining sugar. Cut vents in the top for steam to escape. Bake at 350 degrees for one hour or until filling is bubbly. Makes 6 to 8 servings.

Crust:

4 c. all-purpose flour

1 T. sugar

2 t. salt

1-3/4 c. shortening

1 T. vinegar

1 egg

1/2 c. water

Combine dry ingredients; cut in shortening and add remaining ingredients. Chill for one to 2 hours. Divide dough in half and roll out one at a time. Place bottom into a 9" pie pan.

135

My friend Carol and I started junior high together, longer ago than either of us will admit! We quickly became best friends through high school, summer days at the lake and laughing over our books in college. Afterward, Carol married and started a family and I went to graduate school. We may not have seen each other for months but when we did, it was as if one of us had just gone for a quick trip.

Our lives held many of the same events like marriage, children and career changes, but they were always in a different order. Through it all, Carol and I remained close as ever. She even kept me company when I drove a truck home after cleaning out my father's house. We talked for the entire 14 hours on the road!

Although I'm supposed to be the "foodie" of the pair, this warming, delicious soup is Carol's recipe.

Sandy Lentz
Oak Park, IL

Remember When

Carol's Chunky Minestrone

2 T. olive oil
1-1/2 c. onion, chopped
1 carrot, peeled, halved lengthwise and sliced
1 clove garlic, minced
1/2 c. prepared rice
1/2 t. dried basil
1/2 t. dried oregano
28-oz. can diced tomatoes

14-1/2 oz. can chicken broth
1 zucchini, halved lengthwise and sliced
16-oz. can cannelini beans, drained
salt and pepper to taste
Garnish: grated Parmesan cheese

Heat oil in a Dutch oven over medium heat. Add onion, carrot and garlic; sauté for 3 minutes. Add the next 5 ingredients; cook for 5 minutes. Add remaining ingredients, except cheese; simmer for 10 minutes until soup is blended and heated through. Serve topped with grated Parmesan cheese. Serves 4.

For You!

I have known MarJean for about 10 years and we have become sisters at heart. Last summer, she entered a drawing at one of the local car dealerships and won a trip for two to Hawaii! When she invited me to go along with her, I was thrilled.

We had a blast! We swam, went sightseeing and let the stress of everyday life ease away. I'm so grateful she's my friend. Here's a recipe that quickly became a favorite of ours when we first tasted it.

Virginia Empie
St. George, UT

Remember When

Cranberry-Spinach Salad

1 T. butter
3/4 c. blanched, slivered almonds
1 lb. spinach, rinsed and torn
1 c. sweetened, dried cranberries
2 T. toasted sesame seeds

2 T. poppy seed
1/2 c. sugar
2 t. onion, minced
1/4 t. paprika
1/4 c. white wine vinegar
1/2 c. oil

In a medium saucepan, melt butter over medium heat. Sauté almonds in butter until lightly toasted; remove from heat, drain and let cool. In a large bowl, toss the spinach with the toasted almonds and cranberries. In a medium bowl, whisk together sesame seeds, poppy seed, sugar, onion, paprika, vinegar and oil. Toss with spinach mixture just before serving. Serves 8 to 10.

There is nothing better than the encouragment of a good friend.

-Katherine Hathaway

For You!

My cousin, Sheri is my best friend. She lives in Pennsylvania...we don't get to see each other as often as we'd like so I decided to make a trip to visit her. After I arrived, we sat at the kitchen table, gabbing as usual, and then she pulled out a cheeseball to snack on. I usually don't like cheeseballs, but Sheri said she'd made this one just for me so I tried it.

It was so delicious! We sat there eating and talking and soon half the cheeseball was gone! I hope you enjoy this recipe as much as I do.

Kelly Jewell
Colonial Beach, VA

Remember When

Sheri's Cheeseball

Using a wooden spoon, mix together all ingredients, except walnuts. Shape into a ball and roll in walnuts. Place in an airtight container and chill for 4 hours. Serve with crackers. Serves 6.

Ingredients:

- 8-oz. pkg. cream cheese, softened
- 1 T. mustard
- 1 T. catsup
- 1 T. prepared horseradish
- 8-oz. pkg. shredded sharp Cheddar cheese
- 1/2 c. walnuts, ground

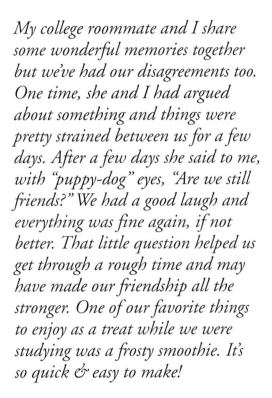

My college roommate and I share some wonderful memories together but we've had our disagreements too. One time, she and I had argued about something and things were pretty strained between us for a few days. After a few days she said to me, with "puppy-dog" eyes, "Are we still friends?" We had a good laugh and everything was fine again, if not better. That little question helped us get through a rough time and may have made our friendship all the stronger. One of our favorite things to enjoy as a treat while we were studying was a frosty smoothie. It's so quick & easy to make!

Shauna Young
Midvale, UT

Remember When

Pineapple-Orange Smoothie

1/4 c. sugar

1 c. vanilla ice cream, softened

1/2 c. water

3 c. ice cubes

8-oz. can frozen pineapple-orange juice concentrate, thawed

Combine all ingredients in a blender; blend until smooth. Makes one to 2 servings.

On a cold December day in 1961, my best friend, Rena Jackson, and I decided we were going to get a Christmas tree. We lived in the country and began to search the woods on my Grandfather's farm...I was 5 years old and Rena was 7.

We got all bundled up and, without telling anyone what we were up to, we headed for the woods where we found two perfect trees. We cut and cut and, from time to time, I'd stand on the tree and jump up and down to help break it off. Finally, we had our trees.

We headed home, each of us dragging a big evergreen tree behind us. Needless to say our parents were very surprised! We soon decorated our trees and thought they were the most beautiful in the world.

Yolanda Dix
Murray, KY

Slow-Cooker Dressing

2 10-3/4 oz. can cream of
   chicken soup
2 14-oz. cans chicken
   broth
1-1/2 t. dried sage
1/2 t. pepper
7-oz. pkg. cornbread mix,
   prepared and crumbled

8 slices white bread, dried
   and crumbled
4 eggs
1 onion, chopped
1/2 c. celery, chopped
2 T. butter

Combine soup, broth, sage and pepper; mix in all other
ingredients, except butter. Spray the bottom and sides of
the slow cooker with non-stick vegetable spray; pour in
dressing. Dot with butter. Cook for 2-1/2 hours on high
or 4 hours on low. Makes 8 to 10 servings.

Where there are friends,
There is wealth.

-Plautus

For You!

A few years ago, two friends and I decided we were going to train for and run in a marathon. Our other friends thought we were crazy! Women in their late 30's and 40's don't usually tackle such a thing, yet here we were...Katie, Sally and I ready to jump in feet-first. During the four months we trained together, we ran anywhere from 8 to 20 miles daily. Somewhere along the many weeks of blisters, sunscreen, mosquito repellent and endless miles, we got into the habit of bringing a snack along to eat after our run. Knowing we could relax and eat in the shade of a big maple tree kept us motivated many days. We'd enjoy banana bread, pecan muffins or honey-wheat bread, trying to keep the snacks healthy yet tasty. After an especially difficult 12-mile run, Katie pulled a magnificent pie from the cooler. We were so hungry we polished off whole thing! We accomplished our goal and completed the marathon, but it was the time together that strengthened our friendship.

Gayle Wagner
Island Lake, IL

Remember When

Katie's 12-Mile Pie

1 T. cold water
1/4 c. cornstarch
1-1/2 c. water
6-oz. pkg. sugar-free
    strawberry gelatin
4 c. fresh berries

9-inch graham cracker
    pie crust
8-oz. container frozen
    whipped topping,
    thawed

Mix cold water with cornstarch until smooth; set aside.
Bring remaining water to a boil; stir in cornstarch mixture
until thick. Add gelatin, stirring well; fold in berries. Pour
into pie shell and refrigerate until set. Top with whipped
topping. Serves 6 to 8.

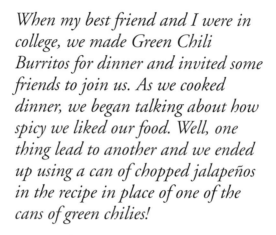

For You!

When my best friend and I were in college, we made Green Chili Burritos for dinner and invited some friends to join us. As we cooked dinner, we began talking about how spicy we liked our food. Well, one thing lead to another and we ended up using a can of chopped jalapeños in the recipe in place of one of the cans of green chilies!

None of us could take a bite without a drink of water and we never tried that substitution again! Now, I live in California and my friend lives in Illinois, but whenever we get together, we make our famous Green Chili Burritos.

Laurie Parrot
La Habra, CA

Remember When

Green Chili Burritos

In an electric skillet, brown cubed pork. Add water, green chilies, flour and garlic powder. Bring to a boil, reduce heat and simmer for one hour. In a separate skillet, brown ground beef; add refried beans and warm throughout. In each tortilla, layer beef mixture, 2 to 3 pieces of pork, a tablespoon of green chili mixture and a sprinkle of onion, black olives and cheese. Roll each tortilla into a burrito and place in a greased 13"x9" baking dish, seam-side down. Pour remaining green chili mixture over the top of burritos and sprinkle on any remaining onions, black olives and cheese. Bake at 350 degrees for 30 to 40 minutes. Garnish with sour cream, if desired. Serves 6 to 8.

Ingredients:

2 lbs. pork, cubed
4 c. water
4 7-oz. cans diced green chilies
2 T. all-purpose flour
1 t. garlic powder
2 lbs. ground beef
31-oz. can refried beans
10-1/2 oz. pkg. flour tortillas
1 onion, chopped
6-oz. can sliced black olives
9-oz. pkg. sharp Cheddar cheese, grated
Garnish: sour cream

For You!

Anytime I hear someone mention cooking and friends, I can't help thinking of my best friend from high school, Susan. One afternoon, I drove to her house and she'd just pulled a cake out of the oven. It was the first cake she'd ever baked and it tasted horrible! Here was a big cake that no one would ever eat...what did we do with it? We buried it in the garden!

I will never forget that cake, but rest assured, this version tastes great!

Donna Rosser
Fayetteville, GA

Remember When

Pistachio Cake

18-1/2 oz. box white
  cake mix
3.4-oz. pkg. instant
  pistachio pudding mix
1 c. oil
3 eggs, beaten

1 c. lemon-lime soda
1 c. slivered almonds,
  toasted and chopped
6-oz. jar cherries, drained
  and chopped

Combine cake and pudding mix; set aside. In a separate bowl, mix together oil, eggs and soda; add to the cake mix, mixing well. Add nuts and cherries. Pour into two greased and floured 9" round cake pans. Bake at 350 degrees for 30 to 35 minutes, or until cake springs back when gently touched. After cooling, spread topping over one layer and stack the other on top; completely cover cake with topping. Serves 8 to 10.

Topping:

3.4-oz. pkg. instant
  pistachio pudding mix
1-1/4 c. milk
6-oz. jar cherries, drained
  and chopped

16-oz. container frozen
  whipped topping,
  thawed
1 c. slivered almonds,
  toasted and chopped

Mix pudding and milk; let stand until set. Add cherries, whipped topping and nuts.

For You!

When we found that we shared a love for flea marketing, we knew our friendship was meant to be! Starting out locally, we eventually began traveling all over the country...tag sales, flea markets and any antique show we could find! Over the years, we've come up with a "system" for combing flea markets together. Jo Ann browses over the whole place first while Vickie falls in love with vintage goodies at first sight! We look for anything that sparks an interest or that we can use in a new way at home. Sure, shopping together is fun but our trips are really about talking, laughing and, of course...eating! For lunch, (gotta have nourishment, y'know!) we always look for a local specialty to sample...southern-style pulled pork is one of our best "finds" yet. This recipe is just like the sandwich we come back to Nashville for every year.

Vickie & Jo Ann

Remember When

Southern-Style Pulled Pork Sandwiches

Heat oil over medium heat; add onions, cooking until soft. Add garlic, chili powder and peppercorns; cook and stir for one minute. Add chili sauce, brown sugar, vinegar, Worcestershire sauce and liquid smoke; bring to a boil, stirring constantly. Place pork in a slow cooker and pour sauce over top. Cover; cook on low setting 10 to 12 hours or on high 6 hours until pork tears easily. Transfer to a cutting board; shred meat with two forks. Return to sauce and keep warm until ready to serve. Warm buns in a 200-degree oven. Makes 8 hearty servings.

Ingredients:

1 T. oil

2 onions, chopped

6 cloves garlic, minced

1 T. chili powder

1 t. cracked black peppercorns

1 c. tomato-based chili sauce

1/4 c. brown sugar, packed

1/4 c. cider vinegar

1 T. Worcestershire sauce

1 t. liquid smoke

3 lbs. boneless pork shoulder

8 onion buns

For You!

Rachel and I became friends before we started kindergarten. Sometimes she'd come over to our home and we'd eat lunch together. All through elementary school we'd get together to play and try new things. One day, Mom gave us a recipe for Peanut Butter Play Dough. We had such fun making it and, after we were done, we ate it! Now, I enjoy making and giving it to some of my little friends.

Joanna Scoresby
Mount Vernon, OH

Remember When

Peanut Butter Play Dough

1-3/4 c. creamy peanut
    butter
2 c. powdered sugar

1-3/4 c. corn syrup
2 c. powdered milk

Mix all ingredients together in a medium bowl.
Makes about 7 cups.

Two years ago, the week before Thanksgiving, everyone where I work decided to have a pie contest. Being a new mother and obsessed with baking, I told my friend I was going to enter the contest. She gave me her full support until she asked what kind of pie I'd be making. I told her I had chosen Peanut Butter Pie. Of course she laughed because that isn't a traditional Thanksgiving dessert. I insisted that variety was the spice of life and I made the pie for the contest. It was a long day spent watching the judges go back and forth as they tasted each. Finally they selected a winner…Peanut Butter Pie! I was so excited! My prize? A traditional Thanksgiving meal. So I guess my friend and I both won that day: her traditional ideas and my fun dessert.

Diane Madej
Amserdam, NY

Remember When

Peanut Butter Pie

In a saucepan, combine butter, milk, sugar and salt; bring to a boil. In a separate bowl, whisk cornstarch and water until smooth; whisk in egg yolks. Pour egg mixture into boiling milk mixture and stir until thick; remove from heat. Add peanut butter, stirring well. Pour into pie shell and chill; top with chocolate syrup and whipped cream, if desired. Serves 6 to 8.

Ingredients:

4 T. butter
2 c. milk
1/3 c. sugar
1/2 t. salt
4 T. cornstarch
1/2 c. water
4 egg yolks
3 T. creamy peanut butter
9-inch pie crust, baked
Garnish: chocolate syrup and whipped topping

For You!

My friend, Marla asked me for this recipe shortly after I met her. She called and asked if there was supposed to be a layer of butter on the bottom of the pan. "Did you put the flour in?" I asked. "What flour?" she said. I had forgotten to add flour to the recipe card when I copied it for her. Needless to say, the cookies are better with flour and we have remained dear friends. By the way...the cookies got their name before I made my error!

Mary Turner
Montrose, CO

Remember When

Grandma's Mistake Bars

Combine oats, flour, sugar, salt and baking soda in a large mixing bowl. Cut in one cup butter to cornmeal consistency; set aside. Melt remaining butter and chocolate chips in a saucepan; add sweetened condensed milk. Pour 3/4 of the oat mixture in the bottom of a lightly greased 13"x9" baking dish. Pour chocolate mixture on top; sprinkle with remaining oat mix. Bake at 350 degrees for 25 minutes. Serves 12.

Ingredients:

- 2 c. quick-cooking oats, uncooked
- 1 c. all-purpose flour
- 1 c. brown sugar, packed
- 1/2 t. salt
- 1/4 t. baking soda
- 1-1/2 c. butter, divided
- 2 c. chocolate chips
- 14-oz. can sweetened condensed milk

Notes

Forever
Friends

Friendships to last a lifetime...

Anne Dickson and I have been friends since first grade. We were inseparable all through school and even attended the same college where we were roommates. We've shared each other's ups & downs and have remained friends even though 1000 miles separate us.

Once a year, we get together and Anne's visit to me is always during Thanksgiving. We shop, laugh, reminisce and bake our famous Butterscotch Cake...yum! The holidays truly start when she walks through my door. I feel very fortunate to have a friend like her.

Stephanie Clancy
McCordsville, IN

Forever Friends

Butterscotch Cake

3-1/2 oz. pkg. cook &
serve butterscotch
pudding mix
1/2 c. oil

18-1/2 oz. box yellow
cake mix
1 c. butterscotch chips

Prepare pudding mix according to package
directions; set aside and cool for 5 minutes.
Combine oil and cake mix; add pudding. Pour into
a greased and floured 13"x9" baking dish. Sprinkle
butterscotch chips on top. Bake at 350 degrees for
30 to 35 minutes. Makes 10 to 12 servings.

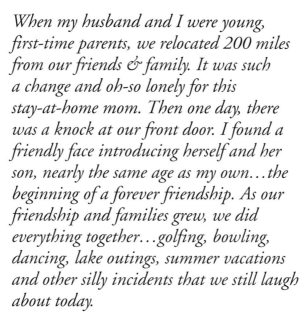

When my husband and I were young, first-time parents, we relocated 200 miles from our friends & family. It was such a change and oh-so lonely for this stay-at-home mom. Then one day, there was a knock at our front door. I found a friendly face introducing herself and her son, nearly the same age as my own…the beginning of a forever friendship. As our friendship and families grew, we did everything together…golfing, bowling, dancing, lake outings, summer vacations and other silly incidents that we still laugh about today.

Time has brought many changes and moves away from that friend, but we still keep in touch and will always be close in our hearts. It seems that the one recipe I remember most from our get-togethers is the one I still love…Italian Roast Beef.

Nicki Baltz
Zionsville, IN

Forever Friends

Italian Roast Beef

Mix shortening with cheese, parsley, garlic, salt, peppers and oregano. Make slits in rump roast and stuff mixture into slits; place in a 6-quart roasting pan. Add water and roast at 325 degrees for 3 to 4 hours. Serves 6 to 8.

Ingredients:

2 T. shortening
2 4-oz. jars grated Romano cheese
1 T. dried parsley
1/8 t. garlic powder
1/8 t. salt
1/8 t. pepper
1/8 t. red pepper
1/8 t. dried oregano
3 to 4-lb. rump roast
2 c. water

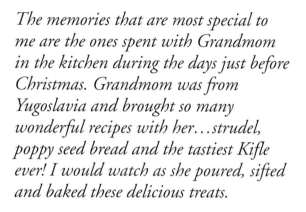

The memories that are most special to me are the ones spent with Grandmom in the kitchen during the days just before Christmas. Grandmom was from Yugoslavia and brought so many wonderful recipes with her…strudel, poppy seed bread and the tastiest Kifle ever! I would watch as she poured, sifted and baked these delicious treats.

As we both grew older, the baking slowed a bit and our time in the kitchen was spent sipping tea and talking about life. Unknowingly, I was learning a very important family matter…grandmothers are a wealth of wondrous knowledge and while you are sitting there enjoying her baked goods, you will soon find that you are treasuring life with a very special friend.

Joyce Hayes
Atco, NJ

Forever Friends

Kifle

Combine cream cheese, butter and flour;
refrigerate overnight. Roll dough out on a
floured surface to pie-crust thickness. Using a
pastry wheel, cut into 3-inch squares. Fill each
with 1/2 teaspoon preserves, jelly or crushed
nuts. Bring two corners together, making a
triangle; pinch sides together. Place on a
lightly greased baking sheet; bake at
400 degrees for 7 to 10 minutes or until
golden. Sprinkle with powdered sugar when
cooled. Makes 8 dozen.

Ingredients:

1/2 lb. cream
cheese, softened

1/2 lb. butter,
softened

2 c. all-purpose
flour

1/3 c. apricot
preserves

1/3 c. prune jelly

1/3 c. crushed nuts

Garnish: powdered
sugar

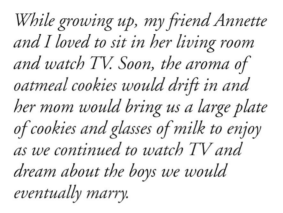

While growing up, my friend Annette and I loved to sit in her living room and watch TV. Soon, the aroma of oatmeal cookies would drift in and her mom would bring us a large plate of cookies and glasses of milk to enjoy as we continued to watch TV and dream about the boys we would eventually marry.

Years later, when my sister hosted a bridal shower and invited all my friends, she asked each to bring a copy of their favorite recipe to share. Annette brought the recipe for the oatmeal cookies we had enjoyed while growing up and now, whenever I bake them, I take time to sit down and dream about the boy I eventually married.

Elizabeth Weingart
Louisville, OH

Forever Friends

Oatmeal Friendship Cookies

3/4 c. shortening
1 c. brown sugar,
    packed
1 egg
1/4 c. water
1 t. vanilla extract

1 c. all-purpose flour
1 t. salt
1/2 t. baking soda
3 c. quick-cooking oats,
    uncooked

Combine first 5 ingredients; beat until creamy.
Sift together flour, salt and baking soda; add to
creamed mixture; blend well. Stir in oats. Drop by
teaspoonfuls onto a greased baking sheet. Bake at
350 degrees for 12 to 15 minutes. Makes 5 dozen.

When Mom went to the hospital the day my sister Julie was born, our very kind neighbors, the Cobriniks, invited us to stay at their home. The movie Mary Poppins had just been released so we all piled into the car to go see it…no small feat since I was one of 5 children and the Cobriniks had 3 of their own! After the movie was over, we drove to the hospital. Mom's room was on the ground floor, so all of us kids peeked in the window while she held up our new baby sister Julie for us all to see and admire.

During our many visits to the Cobriniks' home, who were of Russian-Jewish heritage, we were treated to delicious, special dishes like borscht, meat balls, matzo ball soup and Crispy Potato Pancakes. What wonderful neighbors and friends to have…they always went out of their way for us and gave our family many lasting, happy memories.

Gail Bamford
Bethesda, MD

Forever Friends

Crispy Potato Pancakes

4 potatoes, peeled
  and grated
1 onion, grated
1 egg, beaten

1 t. salt
2 T. all-purpose flour
pepper to taste
2 c. oil

Combine potatoes and onion in a large bowl; drain away any excess liquid. Mix in egg, salt, flour and pepper. If necessary, add more flour to make mixture thick. Heat oil in the bottom of a heavy skillet over medium heat. Drop 1/4 cup potato mixture into hot oil and flatten to make 1/2-inch thick pancakes. Fry until golden brown; flip to fry both sides. Transfer to plates lined with paper towel to drain. Keep warm in a 200 degree oven until serving. Repeat with remaining potato mixture. Makes 2 to 3 servings.

The road to
a friend's house
is never long.

-Danish proverb

Several years ago, I worked in a wonderful country shop. There I met a few ladies who loved so many of the same things I did. We started getting together once a month to share our needlework and craft skills, eat a delicious meal and catch up on what was going on in each of our lives. The group became known as the Heart & Hand and, sometimes, the crafts were a learning process for all of us and some had hilarious results!

Sadly, the country shop that brought us together is gone now…one of our members has moved away and another works full-time, so our gatherings are few and far between. Still, I look back on those days with such fondness for special friends and special times. This favorite recipe came from one of those joyful get-togethers.

Candy Hannigan
Monument, CO

172

Forever Friends

Pumpkin Soup

Sauté green pepper, onion, parsley and thyme in 2 tablespoons butter. Add tomatoes, pumpkin and chicken broth; simmer for one hour and cool. In several small batches, puree mix in a food processor until smooth. In a large stockpot, melt remaining butter; stir in flour until well blended. Stir in milk; continue stirring until slightly thickened. Add pumpkin mixture; simmer for 15 minutes. Season with salt and pepper; serve with leaf croutons. Serves 8.

Leaf Croutons:

8 slices white or wheat bread

3 T. butter, melted

Using a small leaf-shaped cookie cutter, cut out croutons from slices of bread. Place on a baking sheet and brush with melted butter. Bake at 375 degrees for 5 to 10 minutes or until crisp.

Ingredients:

1 green pepper, chopped

1 onion, chopped

4 t. fresh parsley, chopped

1/2 t. dried thyme

4 T. butter, divided

2 15-oz. cans tomatoes

2 15-oz. cans pumpkin

2 14-1/2 oz. cans chicken broth

2 T. butter

1/4 c. all-purpose flour

2 c. milk

salt and pepper to taste

Janice and I met in the 10th grade. We soon learned we had a lot in common...our first and middle names, our birthdays fell just a few days apart and we both had brown hair and green eyes. We quickly became best friends and, once a week, I'd walk home with Janice after school. Her mom would join us at their kitchen table for a snack and to talk about the day's events. Occasionally, my after-school visit would fall on bread-making day.

I listened as her mom explained each step of the process and soon, I was trying my own hand at it. Over the years I've tried a number of different recipes and, often, I still make bread the old-fashioned way, the way Janice's mom taught me...two kneadings and two risings. When time is short, I whip up this Casserole Bread instead. Just the smell of baking bread takes me back to that warm kitchen and my after-school visits with Janice and her mom.

Janice Leffew
Seattle, WA

Forever Friends

Casserole Bread

2 pkgs. active dry yeast
2 c. warm water
2 T. sugar
2 t. salt
2 T. butter
4 c. all-purpose flour, divided

Dissolve yeast in warm water; cover and let set for
10 minutes. Stir in remaining ingredients, except one
cup flour; beat until smooth. Add remaining flour; cover
in a warm place and let dough double in bulk. Stir down,
then beat for 30 seconds. Turn into a greased 1-3/4 quart
baking dish; bake at 375 degrees for 50 to 60 minutes or
until golden and center tests done. Brush top with melted
butter. Makes 4 servings.

My cousin Lynn was also my best friend, and spending the night at her house over the summer was almost as exciting as Christmas to me! Her mother always made the visit even more special by baking chocolate chip cookies. Lynn and I tried to eat as many as we could before they had a chance to cool (or before her brother Rick could devour all of them!). Of all the chocolate chip cookies I've ever had, hers were the best, hands down.

Several years later, I asked Lynn for her mom's recipe so that I could carry on the chocolate chip cookie tradition with my own children. Wondering if her cookies really were the best or if it was merely nostalgia, before the first batch had a chance to cool, I had my answer…they were still the best!

Angela Pike
Hodgenville, KY

Forever Friends

The Best Chocolate Chip Cookies

Cream together sugar and shortening; add egg, mixing well by hand until sugar is dissolved. In a separate bowl, sift dry ingredients together; stir into egg mixture. Add chocolate chips and pecans. Drop by tablespoonfuls onto a greased baking sheet. Bake at 375 degrees for 8 minutes, or until lightly golden on top. Makes 3 dozen.

Ingredients:

1 c. brown sugar, packed

3/4 c. shortening

1 egg

2 c. all-purpose flour

1/2 t. cream of tartar

1/2 t. salt

1/2 t. baking soda

6-oz. pkg. semi-sweet chocolate chips

3/4 c. chopped pecans

The joy of friendship is my best friend Pamela, who I met at 13 years of age and who has remained my best friend for 33 years. Through the years, we've shared laughter and tears, broken hearts, sleepovers, rock & roll, seeing Elvis in concert after my 19th birthday and watching John Wayne movies over and over.

In 33 years, we've never had an argument. We share a mutual love of family, home, faith and values. We love baking, going out to breakfast together and then shopping afterward! This recipe is one Pamela shared with me several years ago; in honor of her, I've re-named it Friendship Casserole.

Brenda Dickson
Overland Park, KS

Forever Friends

Friendship Casserole

2 lbs. stew meat, cubed
1 onion, chopped
2 T. shortening
1 c. water
2 potatoes, sliced
10-3/4 oz. can cream of
    mushroom soup
1-1/4 c. milk

1 c. sour cream
1 t. salt
1/2 t. pepper
1/4 c. whole-grain rice flake
    cereal, crushed
1 c. shredded Cheddar
    cheese

Heat meat, onion and shortening in a large skillet over
medium heat until browned. Add water; heat to a boil.
Reduce heat; cover and simmer for 50 minutes. Pour into a
13"x9" baking dish; arrange potatoes over meat and set
aside. In a mixing bowl, combine soup, milk, sour cream,
salt, and pepper; pour over potatoes. Bake uncovered at
350 degrees for one hour. Remove dish from oven and top
with cereal and cheese. Bake another 30 minutes. Makes
6 to 8 servings.

As a young girl and teenager, I attended countless slumber parties. With two younger sisters and lots of girlfriends from school, there always seemed to be a birthday to celebrate. I remember non-stop giggles, movies, plenty of junk food and the ultimate goal...staying up as late as possible!

Whenever the party was at our house, Mom would help all of us make these Baby Pizzas. We'd have so much fun eating our own creations. This recipe was always a favorite of mine...I make it for my own children now!

Cathy Galicia
Pacifica, CA

Forever Friends

Baby Pizzas

12-oz. tube
  refrigerated biscuits

8-oz. can tomato sauce

10 slices Mozzarella or
  Cheddar cheese

10 slices pepperoni
  or salami

2-1/4 oz. can sliced
  black olives

Place biscuits on an ungreased cookie sheet; flatten slightly. Spoon one tablespoon of sauce on each biscuit; top with remaining ingredients. Bake according to biscuit directions. Makes 10 pizzas.

Best friends since grade school, Kim and I were always there for each other through birthdays, holiday celebrations, school dances, parties, first kisses and boyfriends. She was there for me when I lost my younger sister and I was there for her when her home burned down. We played together as children, hung out together as teens and grew up together along the way. Through these years, we created a lifetime of special memories.

One of those memories includes Kim's love of baking. As a bridal shower gift to me, my mother gathered favorite recipes from family & friends. As matron of honor, Kim contributed a few recipes to the collection, but there is one that I cherish the most because it reminds me of our friendship...one that's simple, but true. As time goes by, we don't spend as much time with each other as we'd like to, but every time we do, it's as if no time has passed at all. We are forever friends.

Kathy Miles
Baltimore, MD

Creamy Coconut Cake

18-1/2 oz. box yellow
   cake mix

1 c. milk

1/2 c. sugar

1-1/2 c. flaked coconut,
   divided

12-oz. container frozen
   whipped topping,
   thawed

Prepare cake mix as directed; bake in a 13"x9" baking dish.
Poke small holes in the cake surface with a fork. Bring milk,
sugar and 1/2 cup coconut to a boil; spread over cake. Frost
with whipped topping and top with remaining coconut.
Refrigerate overnight. Serves 10 to 12.

Thumbing through the index cards in my little wooden recipe box is more than just a search for something good to eat. Among those smudged and often yellowed cards there's a history of family & friends.

Very well represented in that box is my friend of nearly 25 years. Although she is very good at anything she does in the kitchen, Eleanor really shines when it comes to baking. Who could count the many ups & downs we've shared over a plate of her treats? The supply never seems to run out; a few extras are sent when you leave and many are the care packages she has wrapped and sent to friends and relatives.

Making one of her recipes always brings back a flood of warm memories. Brownie Pie is a delicious treat from the oven and was a favorite of my daughters when they were growing up.

Pat Ockert
Jonesboro, AR

Forever Friends

Brownie Pie

1-oz. sq. unsweetened
   baking chocolate

1/2 c. margarine

1 c. sugar

2 eggs, beaten

1/2 c. all-purpose flour

1/8 t. salt

1 t. vanilla extract

Optional: 1/2 c. chopped
   nuts

Melt baking chocolate and margarine together; stir in
remaining ingredients. Pour into a greased 9" pie pan.
Bake at 350 degrees for 30 minutes. Serves 6 to 8.

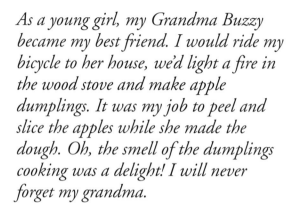

As a young girl, my Grandma Buzzy became my best friend. I would ride my bicycle to her house, we'd light a fire in the wood stove and make apple dumplings. It was my job to peel and slice the apples while she made the dough. Oh, the smell of the dumplings cooking was a delight! I will never forget my grandma.

Sharon Lee Phillips
Bend, OR

Forever Friends

Apple Dumplings

2 c. all-purpose flour
1/2 t. salt
2/3 c. shortening
2 to 3 T. cold water

6 tart apples, cored
and peeled
1/2 c. sugar
1-1/2 t. cinnamon

Combine flour and salt in a mixing bowl; cut in shortening to cornmeal consistency. Add water. Roll dough out on a floured surface; cut into 6 squares large enough to cover each apple. Set an apple in the center of each square. Mix together remaining ingredients; sprinkle over each apple. Bring sides of dough together to cover apples; place seam-side down in a greased 13"x9" baking dish. Pour syrup over dumplings. Bake at 500 degrees for 5 to 7 minutes. Reduce heat to 350; continue baking for 30 to 35 minutes. Serves 6.

Syrup:

1 c. sugar
2 c. water

4 t. butter
1/2 t. cinnamon

Melt all ingredients together in a saucepan over medium heat.

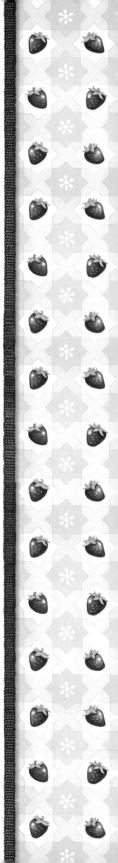

I have fond memories of making Pound Cake with my mother. For as long as I can remember, everyone has looked forward to it at Christmastime!

This recipe was passed down from previous generations to Mom, who was my most faithful best friend.

Ellen Hickey
Nutley, NJ

The best thing
to give a friend
is your heart.

-Francis Maitland Balfour

Forever Friends

Pound Cake

1 c. shortening
4 T. butter
3 c. sugar
5 eggs
1-1/2 T. vanilla extract

3 c. all-purpose flour
1/2 t. baking powder
1/8 t. salt
1 c. milk

Cream shortening, butter and sugar; beat in eggs, one at a time. Add vanilla. In a separate bowl, combine flour, baking powder and salt. Beat into butter mix, alternating with milk. Pour into a greased 10" Bundt® pan; bake at 325 degrees for one hour and 15 minutes. Frost if desired. Serves 10 to 12.

Frosting:

1/4 c. shortening
2-1/2 c. powdered sugar
1/2 t. salt

1/2 t. vanilla extract
1/3 c. milk

Combine all ingredients until creamy.

I grew up with five special friends and we have so many memories...slumber parties, church beach trips, drill team, secrets and a few sorrows. We've stayed close through the years and even attended the same college.

Even though we've married, moved apart and started our own families, there is a special bond between us that will last forever. We get together once each year and have a wonderful time catching up on each other's lives, laughing over old photographs and sharing recipes like this one for Easy Stuffed Mushrooms. We know one of the many blessings in life is friendship and we will continue to cherish ours.

Joy Diomede
Double Oak, TX

Forever Friends

Easy Stuffed Mushrooms

Remove stems from mushrooms. Brush caps with melted butter; fill each with cheese. Bake at 350 degrees for 20 minutes, or until mushrooms are tender. Makes 2 dozen.

Ingredients:

- 2 8-oz. containers whole mushrooms
- 2 T. butter, melted
- 2 5.2-oz. boxes garlic and herb cheese

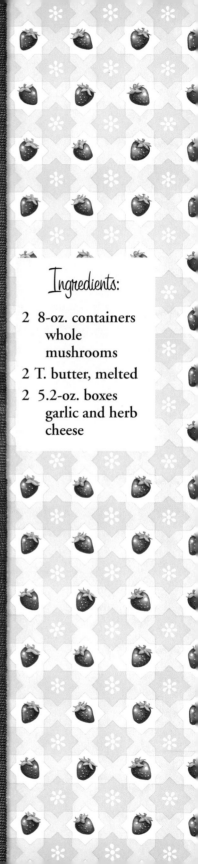

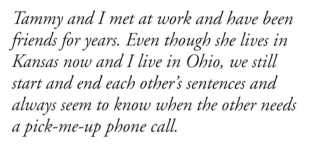

Tammy and I met at work and have been friends for years. Even though she lives in Kansas now and I live in Ohio, we still start and end each other's sentences and always seem to know when the other needs a pick-me-up phone call.

One year, as we prepared for a company Christmas party, we called each other to describe the new outfits we'd both bought. As I began describing my dress, the other end of the phone was quiet...Tammy had bought the exact same dress! Without hesitation she said, "I'll wear something else," and she insisted I wear the new dress. I couldn't imagine anyone being so thoughtful. Now, when I go back to Kansas and we get together, it's like we've never been apart. Our friendship is one I'll always cherish.

Angie Venable
Gooseberry Patch

Forever Friends

Sawdust Potatoes

In a medium saucepan, mix together first 6 ingredients; heat until blended. Stir in hashbrowns; pour mixture into a greased 13"x9" baking dish. Cover and bake at 350 degrees for 40 minutes. In a small mixing bowl, combine bread crumbs and butter; pour over potatoes. Cover and bake for 20 minutes or until golden. Makes 6 to 8 servings.

Ingredients:

10-3/4 oz. can cream of mushroom soup

1/2 c. butter

8-oz. pkg. pasteurized process cheese spread

1/2 c. sour cream

1/4 t. pepper

1/8 t. celery salt

2-lb. pkg. frozen hashbrowns, thawed

1-1/2 c. bread crumbs

2 to 3 T. butter, melted

Close friendships can have their beginnings in the most unexpected ways. My friendship with Ana began 44 years ago when our families met on a ship sailing to Germany.

Our paths crossed many times before we settled permanently in the same area. We have so much in common...a love of cooking, home and family. We have shared much laughter, a few tears and always a shoulder on which to lean and an ear that listens. I am so blessed to be able to say, "She is my friend."

Ethel Bolton
Bienna, VA

Forever Friends

Ana's Natilla

1/4 c. cornstarch

1/2 c. water

12-oz. can evaporated
   milk

2 c. milk

3/4 c. plus 2 T. sugar,
   divided

1/2 t. salt

3 egg yolks, slightly
   beaten

1 t. vanilla extract

3 T. butter

2 T. sugar

Dissolve cornstarch in water. Combine all ingredients, except 2 tablespoons sugar, over low heat, stirring constantly until thickened. Remove from heat; pour into a 2-quart baking dish. Sprinkle remaining sugar evenly over the top and broil until golden. Cool before serving. Serves 4 to 6.

Mama has always been my best friend. I have fond memories of snowy days spent baking special treats with her when I was young.

A family favorite was always her birthday pound cake. Back then, before stand mixers, this cake was a two-person job! One of us would beat the eggs while the other gathered all the other ingredients. We always used a big, green Fire-King bowl to mix the cake in and, later on, Mama gave it to me...I treasure it. Served with fruit, ice cream or frosted, this cake has been loved by four generations of our family over the last 40 years.

Rhonda Jones
Rocky Mount, VA

Mama's Pound Cake

7 eggs
2 c. sugar
1-1/2 c. margarine, melted

2 c. self-rising flour
2 t. vanilla extract

Beat eggs in a large bowl for 20 minutes until foamy; set aside. Cream sugar and margarine. Alternate adding margarine mix and flour to eggs, mixing well. Add vanilla extract. Pour into a greased Bundt® pan; bake at 325 degrees for one hour or until golden. Serves 10 to 12.

Growing up, my very special friend was my Grammy. She lived with us for ten years when she first came to America from Hungary in 1946. Our best times together were when she would cook or bake. I was always fascinated because she never used a recipe and could whip up anything!

I learned her recipes by watching and touching. She made many comfort foods, but the greatest comfort was her friendship of sharing, caring and spending time with me. This is one of the special treats she often shared with me.

Susie Knupp
Somers, MT

Forever Friends

Grammy's Hungarian Nut Rolls

3 c. all-purpose flour
1/2 lb. margarine, softened

8-oz. pkg. cream cheese
Garnish: powdered sugar

Mix all ingredients to form dough; pinch off dough into 50 balls. Refrigerate overnight. Roll each out on a surface dusted with powdered sugar. Fill with a teaspoon of nut filling; fold over to form a half circle. Bake at 350 degrees, on an ungreased baking sheet, for 20 to 25 minutes. Cool and sprinkle with powdered sugar. Makes 4 dozen.

Nut Filling:

3 egg whites
1/2 c. sugar

1 lb. walnuts, ground
1/4 t. vanilla extract

Beat egg whites until stiff; add sugar and beat. Fold in nuts and vanilla.

I'm writing to tell you about a longtime friendship. My friend, Louise, and I were born in the same year: 1916. Our mothers were even friends for many years before we were born. We both can remember the end of World War I…we started school together and grew up in the rural farming community of Flint, Georgia. We attended the same college and both became teachers, married, had families but eventually moved to different towns. Even though we don't see each other often, we've kept in touch. Eighty-five years is a long, enduring friendship that's filled with many, many memories.

Sara Willis
Marietta, GA

Forever Friends

Fresh Peach Pie

1 c. sugar

3 T. flour

1/8 t. cinnamon

9-inch pie crust,
    unbaked

6 to 7 peaches, pitted,
    peeled and sliced

2 T. butter

Combine sugar, flour, cinnamon in a small mixing bowl; sprinkle half of mixture over unbaked crust. Arrange peaches in a single layer over mixture; sprinkle remaining sugar mixture over peaches and dot with butter. Bake at 400 degrees for one hour. Serves 6 to 8.

I started my first real job in 1965 while I was still in high school. A green recruit at best, I worked in an office after school with 15 women of various ages. As the only male among so many females, I was a little intimidated by the situation to say the least!

I soon made friends however, and one of those friendships was with Elsie. She was about the age of my mother and was in charge of a particular subscription list that I printed. Each address had to be stamped on the wrapper, which I did using an outdated stamping machine. I found that each time after I ran her lists, she would bake her famous Oatmeal-Chocolate Cake for me.

Elsie passed away about 20 years ago, but each time I bake this cake, it brings back memories of Elsie and how she helped me to feel at home at my first job.

Stephen Crane
Fair Grove, MO

Elsie's Chocolate-Oatmeal Cake

1 c. quick-cooking oats, uncooked
1-1/2 c. boiling water
1/2 c. shortening
1/2 c. sugar
2 eggs

1 c. all-purpose flour, sifted
1/2 c. baking cocoa
1 t. baking soda
1/2 t. salt
1 t. vanilla extract

Mix oats and boiling water; set aside and let stand for 20 minutes. In a separate bowl, cream shortening, sugar and eggs; add oatmeal mixture and remaining ingredients, beating until smooth. Pour into a greased 13"x9" baking dish; bake at 350 degrees for 30 minutes. Pour topping over cake while still warm and return to the oven for several minutes until lightly golden. Serves 12 to 16.

Topping:

1/4 c. milk
1/2 c. brown sugar, packed

6 t. butter
1 c. flaked coconut

Combine all ingredients, blending well.

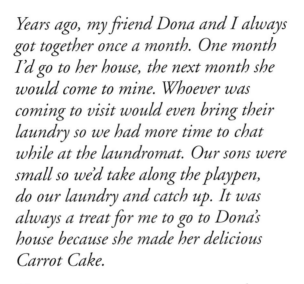

Years ago, my friend Dona and I always got together once a month. One month I'd go to her house, the next month she would come to mine. Whoever was coming to visit would even bring their laundry so we had more time to chat while at the laundromat. Our sons were small so we'd take along the playpen, do our laundry and catch up. It was always a treat for me to go to Dona's house because she made her delicious Carrot Cake.

Our sons are grown men now and Dona and I don't see each other as much as we'd like to, but every time I make this cake, I think of her and the great times we've had.

Shari Miller
Hobart, IN

Forever Friends

Carrot Cake

2 c. all-purpose flour
2 t. cinnamon
2 t. baking powder
1/2 t. baking soda
1-1/2 c. oil

2 c. sugar
4 eggs
2 c. carrots, grated
15-1/4 oz. can crushed
   pineapple, drained

Sift first 4 ingredients together; mix in remaining ingredients. Pour into a greased and floured 13"x9" baking pan; bake at 350 degrees for 35 to 40 minutes. Frost with cream cheese frosting. Serves 10 to 12.

Cream Cheese Frosting:

1/2 c. margarine,
   softened
8-oz. pkg. cream cheese,
   softened

1-lb. pkg. powdered
   sugar
1 t. vanilla extract

Combine all ingredients; beat until smooth.

Kim Smith and I met in kindergarten, 37 years ago. Almost immediately, we became very good friends and have remained best friends ever since. We've shared so many experiences together, I can't imagine my life without her.

Kim moved to a different town when we were both in junior high, but even then, we kept in touch. We celebrated our high school graduations, were in each other's weddings and even worked together for 12 years. Together we've been through the the birth of Kim's children and the death of loved ones. The greatest honor she and her husband bestowed upon my husband and me was asking us to be their daughter's godparents. Through all the years, Kim and I have never spoken a cross word so, in her honor, I would like to share a recipe she shared with me.

Cindy Kozar
Ruffsdale, PA

Forever Friends

Kim's Cucumber Salad

1/2 lb. rigatoni pasta,
    cooked and drained
1 T. oil
2 cucumbers, thinly sliced
1 onion, sliced
1-1/2 c. sugar
3/4 c. vinegar

1 T. dried parsley flakes
1 t. pepper
1 c. water
1 t. dry mustard
1 t. salt
1/2 t. garlic salt

Rinse pasta with cold water; place in a large mixing bowl. Stir in oil, cucumbers and onion; set aside. In a separate bowl, combine remaining ingredients; pour over salad, tossing well. Cover and chill 3 to 4 hours, stirring occasionally. Serves 4 to 6.

One cold, North Carolina day I was dreading doing anything outside when my doorbell rang. I went to the door and found my dearest friend standing there with two mugs of hot Friendship Tea.

Even though we now live apart (she lives in Germany and I live in New York), she still manages to send me this wonderful tea mix. It's truly earned the name because, whenever I make it, I remember our fun times together and wish for more.

Anne Bentley
Ft. Drum, NY

Forever Friends

Rochelle & Anne's Friendship Tea

Combine all ingredients in a large bowl, stirring well. Store in an airtight container. To serve, place 1-1/2 teaspoons mix into one cup boiling water; stir well. Makes 4-1/2 cups dry mix.

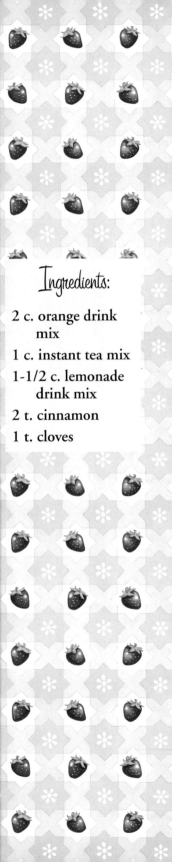

Ingredients:

2 c. orange drink mix

1 c. instant tea mix

1-1/2 c. lemonade drink mix

2 t. cinnamon

1 t. cloves

To say that Julie and I grew up together is a little inaccurate; she was a farm kid and I lived in town. She and I went to the same school together, rode the same bus and have been friends for more than 25 years. Through school, relationships, college and beyond, we've always been there for one another.

Julie lives hundreds of miles away now, but the Information Age has made her only an e-mail away and she's never far from my heart. My oldest and most precious friend gave this cookie recipe to me when were still in high school.

Wendy Whipple
Matteson, IL

Forever Friends

Amish Sugar Cookies

1 c. sugar
1 c. powdered sugar
1 c. margarine
1 c. oil
2 eggs

4-1/2 c. all-purpose
flour
1 t. baking soda
1 t. cream of tartar
1 t. vanilla extract

Cream first 4 ingredients together; add eggs and beat. Mix in remaining ingredients; chill until dough is stiff. Roll dough into one-inch balls and flatten with the bottom of a juice glass that has been pressed into sugar. Place cookies on an ungreased baking sheet; bake at 350 degrees for 10 to 12 minutes or until lightly golden. Makes 3 to 4 dozen.

My dearest, closest friend and I had lunch together last holiday season at a local restaurant to exchange our gifts. She presented me with half a gold charm with the word "Best" engraved on the front and she had the other half...engraved "Friend."

I wear mine daily and this will always be a touching memory for me. It came from a friend I've confided in for over 30 years. Together we've shared weddings, births, new homes, sorrows and raising teenagers. The charm was unexpected, but that is what friendship is too...an unexpected pleasure in our lives.

Jo Anne Hayon
Sheboygan, WI

Truly great friends
are hard to find,
difficult to leave,
and impossible to forget.

-G. Randolf

Forever Friends

Mini Ham Puffs

1 c. water
1/2 c. butter

1 c. all-purpose flour
4 eggs

In a saucepan, heat water and butter to a rolling boil; stir in flour. Continue stirring over low heat until mixture forms a ball; remove from heat. Beat in eggs until mixture turns smooth and glossy. Drop dough by rounded teaspoonfuls onto ungreased baking sheets. Bake at 400 degrees for 25 minutes until golden and dry; cool on wire racks. Just before serving, slice off the top of each puff; remove any fillaments of soft dough. Fill each puff with a rounded teaspoonful of ham filling. Makes 5 to 6 dozen.

Ham Filling:

3 4-1/2 oz. cans deviled
    ham
1 T. prepared horseradish

3/4 t. pepper
3/4 t. salt
1/3 c. sour cream

Blend all ingredients together; refrigerate while puffs bake.

I still remember my very best friend from the third grade! Anne Nielsen and I became fast friends in the third grade and shared many happy times until I moved away during the eighth grade. I have many fond memories of sleepovers at her house.

We'd share a hide-a-bed in her den and giggle into the night. We loved to play jacks and board games. Her mother was a gracious lady and an excellent cook. She baked a cake that makes my tastebuds water just to think about it! I remember eating it many times…I still have the recipe copied on a card in my childish handwriting.

Kirstin Bolander Rich
Sumner, WA

Watergate Cake with Cover-Up Icing

18-1/2 oz. box white
   cake mix
3.4-oz. pkg. instant
   pistachio pudding mix
3 eggs

3/4 c. oil
1 c. lemon-lime soda
3/4 c. flaked coconut
1 c. chopped pecans

Combine first 5 ingredients in a large mixing bowl; beat until well blended. Pour into a greased and floured 13"x9" baking dish; bake at 350 degrees for 45 minutes. Cool and frost. Top with coconut and pecans. Serves 10 to 12.

Icing:

2 1-1/2 oz. pkgs. whipped
   topping mix
1-1/2 c. milk

3.4-oz. pkg. instant
   pistachio pudding mix

Beat all ingredients until smooth.

In 1972, Rita and I met at work where we were both secretaries. We were 18 years old and became instant friends. Our friendship has lasted 29 years.

We've shared both happy and sad times. Rita and her family were there to support my family when my mother and father-in-law passed away. In fact, they drove through a snowstorm to shovel our driveway so we could get in easily when we returned home from an out-of-town funeral.

Each year, we celebrate our birthdays by cooking dinner for each other and our families. This punch is a long-time favorite. I'm on a restricted diet due to health problems, but Rita goes out of her way to make dinner according to my diet. She's very generous and is always offering to help in whatever she can...she's like a sister to me.

Deborah Ocker
Harrisburg, PA

Forever Friends

Mock Champagne Punch

1/2 c. sugar

1 c. water

6-oz. can frozen
   grapefruit juice
   concentrate

6-oz. can frozen orange juice
   concentrate

1/3 c. grenadine syrup

28-oz. bottle ginger ale

Combine sugar and water in a saucepan; boil for 5 minutes, then cool. Add frozen juices and grenadine; refrigerate overnight. Just before serving, add ginger ale. Makes 1-1/2 quarts.

Our lives are filled
with simple joys
and blessings
without end,
and one of the greatest
joys in life is to
have a friend.

-Unknown

When I was 14 years old, my dad moved our family to another state and I had to leave all my teenage friends. Although we visited in the summer and wrote letters, my friends and I gradually grew apart, as happens in life.

After graduation from high school, I returned to my former hometown to attend college. Most of my old friends had chosen to go to school in other places or were busy with their own lives, so we had little contact. On my birthday that year, I was surprised by a knock on the door of my dorm room. When I opened the door, there stood some of my old friends with a wonderful homemade birthday cake. Although life had separated us, they still remembered me and wanted to do something special for me. I was the envy of the entire dorm at that moment!

Margaret Scoresby
Mount Vernon, OH

Golden Layer Cake

2-1/4 c. all-purpose flour
1-1/2 c. sugar
1 t. salt
2-1/2 t. baking powder

2 eggs
1/2 c. shortening
1 t. vanilla extract
1 to 1-1/2 c. milk

Sift dry ingredients together; add remaining ingredients, mixing well. Pour into a greased 13"x9" baking pan. Bake at 350 degrees for 30 to 40 minutes. Cool and frost. Makes 10 to 12 servings.

Chocolate Satin Frosting:

2/3 c. baking cocoa
2/3 c. margarine
3 c. powdered sugar, sifted

2 to 3 t. hot water
1 t. vanilla extract

Combine all ingredients; beat until smooth.

Index

Appetizers

Bread Bowl Dip, 65
Easy Stuffed
  Mushrooms, 191
Mini Ham Puffs, 213
Sheri's Cheeseball, 141

Beverages

Creamy Hot Chocolate
  Mix, 45
Mock Champagne
  Punch, 217
Pineapple-Orange
  Smoothie, 143
Rochelle & Anne's
  Friendship Tea, 209
Simply Delicious
  Lemonade, 121

Breads

Casserole Bread, 175
Christmas Stollen, 129
Homemade Yeast Rolls, 57
Lemon Tea Loaf, 55
No-Knead Rolls, 87
Old-Fashioned Yeast
  Rolls, 33

Breakfast

Bran-Raisin Scones, 73
Cinnamon Rolls, 11

Egg Casserole, 91
Karen's Raisin Scones, 37
Maple Nutty Scones, 119

Candy

Caramel Corn, 69
Chocolate-Covered Peanut
  Butter Balls, 9
Christmas Balls, 29
Earl's Caramel Corn, 7
Nadine's Fudge, 27
Peanut Butter Balls, 131
Twins' Toffee, 81

Cookies

Amish Sugar Cookies, 211
Aunt Lizzie's Forgotten
  Cookies, 99
Chewy Chocolate Chip
  Cookies, 83
Cinnamon Chip
  Cookies, 61
Ginger Cookies, 77
Grandmother's Butter
  Cookies, 23
Grandpa's Favorite
  Oatmeal Cookies, 17
Mid's Imperial Cookies, 31
Norwegian Royal
  Crown Cookies, 19

Index

Oatmeal Friendship
    Cookies, 169
Pineapple Cookies, 127
Snickerdoodles, 125
The Best Chocolate Chip
    Cookies, 177
Vanilla Drop Cookies, 79

Desserts

Almond Banket, 59
Ana's Natilla, 195
Apple Crisp Pizza, 89
Apple Custard Pie, 35
Apple Dumplings, 187
Brownie-Nut Pizza, 21
Brownie Pie, 185
Butterscotch Cake, 163
Carrot Cake, 205
Creamy Coconut Cake, 183
Double Apple Cake, 63
Elsie's Chocolate-Oatmeal
    Cake, 203
Fudgy Brownie Cake, 25
Fresh Peach Pie, 201
Fresh Rhubarb Pie, 135
Fruit Jumbles, 101
Golden Layer Cake, 219
Grammy's Hungarian Nut
    Rolls, 199
Grandma's Mistake Bars, 159
Katie's 12-Mile Pie, 147
Kifle, 167

Lila's Lemon Meringue
    Pie, 51
Mama's Pound Cake, 197
Microwave Banana
    Pudding, 71
Mom's Creme Puffs, 47
Peanut Butter Pie, 157
Pistachio Cake, 151
Pound Cake, 189
Pumpkin Roll, 43
Raspberry-Walnut Cake, 75
Sinfully Delicious
    Brownies, 117
Southern Banana
    Pudding, 13
Watergate Cake with
    Cover-Up Icing, 215

Mains

Baby Pizzas, 181
Barbara's Mission
    Casserole, 15
Barley Casserole, 67
Chicken-Broccoli
    Casserole, 93
Friendship Casserole, 179
Green Chili Burritos, 149
Italian Roast Beef, 165
Kielbasa & Potatoes, 111
Meat Loaf, 103
Mexican Lasagna, 107
Mom's Baked Chicken, 123

Index

Mom's Corned Beef
  Casserole, 97
Shredded Beef
  Sandwiches, 105
Southern-Style Pulled Pork
  Sandwiches, 153
Sunday Chicken, 39

Miscellaneous

Chef's Salt, 95
Fresh Tomato Salsa, 85
Peanut Butter Play
  Dough, 155

Salad

Cranberry-Spinach Salad, 139
Kim's Cucumber Salad, 207
Quick & Easy Vegetable
  Salad, 133
Summertime Pasta Salad, 53
Tortellini Salad, 113

Sides

Crispy Potato Pancakes, 171
June's Potatoes, 109
Pop's Goody Potatoes, 41
Sawdust Potatoes, 193
Slow-Cooker Dressing, 145

Soups

Carol's Chunky
  Minestrone, 137
Pumpkin Soup, 173